KENNETH

ILLUSTRATED BY S

DON'T
KNOW
MUCH
ABOUT®
Sitting
Bull

HarperCollins*Publishers*

This is a Don't Know Much About® book.
Don't Know Much About® is the trademark of Kenneth C. Davis.

Don't Know Much About® Sitting Bull

Copyright © 2003 by Kenneth C. Davis

www.harperchildrens.com

Library of Congress Cataloging-in-Publication Data
Davis, Kenneth C.
    Don't know much about Sitting Bull / Kenneth C. Davis ;
illustrated by Sergio Martinez.— 1st ed.
        p.   cm. — (Don't know much about)
    Includes bibliographical references and index.
    Contents: A boy named Slow — People of the buffalo — Sitting bulls and running horses — Chief Sitting Bull — The hairy men and the Indians — Battles and treaties — How the West was lost — The Battle of the Little Bighorn — The last Indian.
    ISBN 0-06-442125-2 (pbk.) — ISBN 0-06-028818-3 (lib. bdg.)
    1. Sitting Bull, 1834?–1890—Juvenile literature. 2. Dakota Indians—Kings and rulers—Biography—Juvenile literature. 3. Dakota Indians—History—Juvenile literature. 4. Children's questions and answers. [1. Sitting Bull, 1834?–1890. 2. Dakota Indians—Biography. 3. Hunkpapa Indians—Biography. 4. Indians of North America—Great Plains—Biography. 5. Kings, queens, rulers, etc.—Miscellanea. 6. Questions and answers.] I. Martinez, Sergio, ill. II. Title. III. Series: Davis, Kenneth C., Don't know much.
E99.D1 S6023 2003   2002001465
978.004'9752'0092—dc21   CIP
                                                                   AC

Design by Charles Yuen
1 2 3 4 5 6 7 8 9 10

❖

First Edition

ACKNOWLEDGMENTS

An author's name goes on the cover of a book. But behind that book are a great many people who make it all happen. I would like to thank all of the wonderful people at HarperCollins who helped make this book a reality, including Susan Katz, Kate Morgan Jackson, Barbara Lalicki, Harriett Barton, Rosemary Brosnan, Meredith Charpentier, Amy Burton, Dana Hayward, Maggie Herold, Jeanne Hogle, Fumi Kosaka, Rachel Orr, Donna Lifshotz, and Robina Khalid. I would also like to thank David Black, Joy Tutela, and Alix Reid for their friendship, assistance, and great ideas. My wife, Joann, and my children, Jenny and Colin, are always a source of inspiration, joy, and support, and without them my work would not be possible.

I especially thank Jeff Pearson for reviewing the manuscript and providing helpful insights, Sergio Martinez for his beautiful illustrations, and Judy Levin for her hard work and unique contribution.

CONTENTS

When I was a little boy, two of the things that I loved most were western movies and playing Cowboys and Indians. Of course, in the western movies back then, the cowboys and American soldiers were always the "good guys." The Indians in the movies were great fighters who rode horses, shot arrows, painted their faces, and scalped their enemies. And they were almost always the "bad guys."

Nowadays, we know that these old ideas about Native Americans, or "Indians," were mostly myths and legends—exciting stories made up for the movies.

First of all, there were many different kinds of Indians living in different parts of America hundreds of years ago. Among the Plains Indians was a great tribe called the Lakota, a powerful and extraordinary group of people. And one of the proudest of the Lakota was a young boy who was first named Slow, but who later became a great chief known as Sitting Bull. This is the remarkable true story of Sitting Bull, one of the greatest leaders in American history. Although Sitting Bull became famous as a warrior who fought against the United States, he was a leader who wanted what was best for his people and tried to preserve the Lakota way of life.

The true story of the Indians is mostly a very sad story of death, disease, war, and broken promises. That is one reason this is such an important story for us to understand, especially since the truth about Indians like Sitting Bull has been so confused by the movies and television. When Sitting Bull, or

Slow, was born, there were few "whites" (Europeans) in his land and the Lakota was one of the most powerful of tribes. Sixty years later, the Lakota had lost their lands and many of them were dead.

Like all Don't Know Much About® books, this one sets out to tell a story of real people who lived a long time ago. It does that by asking questions. Where was Sitting Bull's home, and what kind of diapers did he wear? Did the Lakota really scalp people? Who won the wars between Sitting Bull and the white settlers who moved out west? And what really

Sitting Bull

happened at the Battle of the Little Bighorn, one of the most famous battles in American history? These questions will help you understand a way of life that is completely different from our modern world.

Along the way, you will read the "Voices" of actual people who lived when Sitting Bull lived. Milestones help explain what else was happening in the world while Sitting Bull led his people.

But the answers to the questions will also show that Indians like Sitting Bull believed in many of the same ideas we think are important today. Being loyal, honest, and brave. Taking care of your family. Taking care of the earth, the most precious thing to the Lakota. And mostly, Sitting Bull fought for the same ideas as George Washington did. He wanted his people to be free. This is his story.

CHAPTER 1

A Boy Named Slow

What was Sitting Bull like as a baby?

When he was born, his name wasn't Sitting Bull. Like most Lakota, Sitting Bull had more than one name during his life. A name says who someone is, so when you do something important or something important happens to you, your name changes.

Sitting Bull was named Jumping Badger when he was born, but soon people called him "Slow." The name wasn't an insult. It meant he was thoughtful, careful, and maybe a little stubborn.

"I was born on the Missouri River," Sitting Bull once said. "At least I recollect that somebody told me so." He doesn't remember what year he was born either. That was not important to the Lakota. Historians think he was born in 1831 or maybe later, in what is now Bullhead, South Dakota.

Were Sitting Bull's parents named Mr. and Mrs. Bull?

Slow's father was named Returns-Again-to-Strike-the-Enemy. He was a respected warrior who owned many horses. His mother was named Mixed-Day (later named Her-Holy-Door), and his older sister was named Many-Feathers. But a Lakota family wasn't just mom and dad and the kids. Slow called all his father's brothers and male cousins "father," too. His mother's sisters and women cousins were his "mothers." A Lakota family was big. And his whole big family was glad to have him. "A child is the greatest gift from Wakantanka [the Great Mysterious]," say the Lakota.

Where was Sitting Bull's home?

Sitting Bull lived in his mother's tipi (women owned the tipis), but "home" was his big family and a few other families they traveled with. They would meet up with other Lakota for part of the summer. In the coldest part of winter, they would choose one place to camp. The rest of the year they followed the buffalo herds. Not just the hunters, everyone. Horses dragged travois loaded with tipis, clothes, food, and buffalo robes. All that moving around was one reason Lakota didn't own much. It's also a reason they loved their land so much. They traveled all over their beautiful land, and it was all home.

> **WHAT DOES IT MEAN?**
>
> A **travois** (tra-VOY) is made of two tipi poles with a leather platform between them.

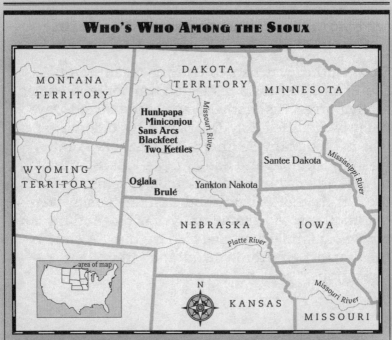

Long before Sitting Bull was born, some of his people's enemies called them "little snakes." The French (who met them before the English did) heard the enemies' word for "little snakes" as *Sioux,* so that's what white people called them. It wasn't what the people called themselves, and it still isn't. They say they are *Lakota,* which means "us people" or "allies" (friends). Lakota is the name of their language, too.

By the time Slow was born, there were Lakota in many places. The Santee farmed and hunted further east, in what is now Minnesota. The Santee say they are *Dakota*. It's the same word, but pronounced differently. (North and South Dakota are named for them.) And there was another group called Yanktons who said *Nakota.*

Slow's people were the Teton Lakota, the western people, and there were seven tribes of them (shown in bold on the map). Slow's family were Hunkpapa, but even the Hunkpapa separated into smaller groups—hunting bands—for part of the year. All three thousand Hunkpapa couldn't travel together.

What was Slow's life like when he was a baby?

Baby Slow stayed in his cradle for most of the first six months or more of his life. It was kind of a deerskin baby-backpack that could be attached to a flat wooden board.

Except at night, when he slept between his parents, Slow didn't spend much time on his back. There were no cribs for Lakota babies. While his mother worked, she could lean the cradleboard on a tree or hang it from a tipi pole. Slow could look straight out—not up—so he could be with his people right from the start, learning to be Lakota. He learned it very well.

AMERICAN VOICES

66 I began to see when I was not yet born; when I was not in my mother's arms, but inside my mother's belly. It was there that I began to study about my people. 99

—Sitting Bull

What kind of diapers did Slow wear?

Slow wore a kind of disposable diaper. His cradle was stuffed with dry moss or animal hair. A little hole at the bottom of the cradle let pee drip out. Slow's mother would wash and oil him and change his moss diaper. He could kick and wiggle then.

After Slow outgrew his cradle, he would wander around with no diaper. In fact, in the summer he wouldn't wear anything at all.

What could Slow see from his cradle?

He watched his mother and the other women scrape buffalo hides with a bone scraper and tan the leather and sew it into robes, clothes, and even new tipis when needed. He watched them cook stew in a bag made from a buffalo's stomach. They put in meat and water and roots and then cooked it by putting hot rocks in. Slow's mother might have had a metal pot if his father had gotten one from a white trader. Slow watched his big sister help the women and play with her doll and toy tipi. He saw the women dig up wild potatoes and onions and he would smell the fresh dirt as they dug. He could see and smell the fire, too. It would be in the middle of the tipi in the winter (the smoke went out a hole in the top) and outside in the summer.

He could smell the family's best horses tethered close to the tipi at night so enemies couldn't steal them. He'd see his father and uncles and cousins fixing arrows and painting buffalo hides. And dogs running everywhere, and people talking everywhere, and singing sometimes and dancing, before and after a battle or a buffalo hunt. In some camps he could see Lakota hunting lands in all directions, all the way to the horizon.

And he could sleep, if he liked, and pee, and do all the things babies do—except cry.

Why didn't Lakota babies cry?

Mothers took their children to a safe place during an enemy attack, and a crying baby might tell the enemy where the family was hiding. Mari Sandoz, a little white girl who grew up with Lakota neighbors, once saw a Lakota friend's new baby brother. When the baby started to cry, its mother pinched its nose closed and covered its mouth for a moment and sang very quietly to it. She would do that again anytime the baby cried. Mari thought this was a great idea. (But she didn't try this with her brothers and sisters, and NEITHER SHOULD YOU. A baby can't breathe with its nose and mouth shut.)

What was Slow's life like when he outgrew his cradle?

When Slow was about six months to a year old, he could start to explore his world by himself. There weren't a lot of rules for a Lakota baby. He could go anyplace he wanted. Whenever he was hungry, someone would feed him. Any mother who was breastfeeding would give him a drink. If he was tired, he could sleep in any tipi. There were no regular bedtimes.

If Slow reached out to touch fire, no one would stop him. Nobody would let a baby get burned up or crawl in front of a charging buffalo, but the Lakota said that babies had to find out about the world for themselves. A burned finger was a good way to learn that fires are hot. (Today, of course, we NEVER let small children near fire!)

How do we know about Sitting Bull and the Lakota?

Lots of ways. Sitting Bull's people believed their history was important. "A people without history is like wind on the buffalo grass," they said. At the end of a battle or a hunt, people would get together and tell all about it until everyone knew what had happened. And if someone lied about his battle deeds, everyone would get mad. Telling and remembering the truth was important to them.

The Lakota didn't write, but they did keep records. Men painted pictures of battles and hunts on their tipis and war shirts and in notebooks they got from traders. Sitting Bull drew pictures of all his important fights. The Lakota also painted a calendar called a "winter count." Each year one event was chosen to name and remember that year: an important battle, a terrible disease, or something unusual like a meteor shower. The pictures helped people recall their history. Someone might remember that "the year the stars fell" was the year he stole six horses from the Crow Indians. (Modern people do the same thing. You might remember that something happened "the same winter I broke my arm." A year is just a number. A broken arm is hard to forget.)

We also have things the Lakota made, like cradleboards, tipis, pipes, war shirts, bows and arrows, and cooking pots. These items show us how people lived and worked.

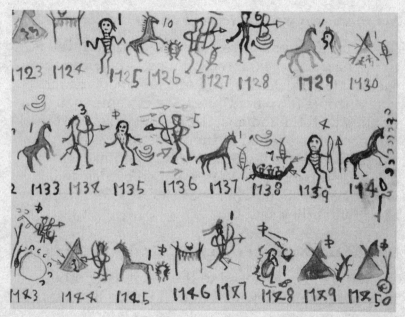

A winter count by Brulé Dakota Battiste Good (1821–ca. 1907)

Are there photographs of Sitting Bull and his people?

Yes, but the camera wasn't invented until 1839. Even then, there were no cameras near the Lakota. So there are pictures of Sitting Bull when he was old but none from when he was young. The photographs of Lakota dancing, working, and hanging out with their families all were taken after Sitting Bull was grown up.

Some painters, like George Catlin, traveled to the Great Plains and painted pictures of Slow's people before Slow was born. Catlin then brought his paintings and writings and some live Indians to show people back east and in other countries.

Are there any written records about the Lakota?

Sure. For hundreds of years, missionaries, travelers, trappers, traders, explorers, and settlers wrote about them in letters, diaries, and official reports. Later, when people from the United States came to make treaties with the Indians, the treaty makers wrote down what happened at their meetings. When the tribes and the United States were fighting each other, newspaper reporters watched battles and wrote stories about what they saw. Soldiers wrote about what they saw, too.

Did the Lakota ever get to tell their side of the story?

Yes. White people talked to the Lakota and other Indian nations. They interviewed Sitting Bull for the newspapers, when he was old. Years later they asked Sitting Bull's family and other men and women to talk about what he was like as a boy and what he did as a chief. They asked about battles and ceremonies and celebrations. Then the white people wrote it all down. Some Lakota went to schools and wrote about their own lives. Charles Eastman was a Santee who became a doctor and wrote about his childhood.

So do we know all about Sitting Bull?

No. Sometimes the history of Sitting Bull and his times sounds like the stories kids tell when the teacher asks what happened in a big fight on the playground. People honestly remember things differently. People stick up for their friends. People are afraid of getting in trouble if they tell the truth. People lie.

Sometimes whites didn't understand the Lakota language very well. Sometimes there isn't even a word in English for a Lakota idea. The whites and the Indians sometimes tell very different stories about the same events. So, all through Sitting Bull's story, we have to look at the pictures and read the stories and try to understand what he was like and what he did.

CHAPTER 2

People of the Buffalo

Lakota tipis in North Dakota

❝ The tipi is much better to live in; always clean, warm in winter, cool in summer; easy to move. Indians and animals know better how to live than white man; nobody can be in good health if he does not have all the time fresh air, sunshine and good water. ❞

—**Flying Hawk**, Lakota chief, (1852–1931)

How much did a tipi cost?

You couldn't buy one, at least not before 1860. Women made them. They scraped and cleaned skins from buffalo that men had shot, and tanned them. Men would sometimes paint the skins with stories of hunts or battles they had fought. Then the women got together and sewed the skins into the tipi (or *lodge*) cover. It took twelve to fourteen skins to make a tipi about fifteen feet across. Men or women would make the lodge poles—the tall poles that supported the tipi cover—from skinny tree trunks. A successful warrior with a big family would have a bigger lodge. He would have more family to live in it, and more family and horses to move it around. The Teton Lakota had to move often, when hunting or when attacked. A few women working together could take down a tipi and pack it and everything in it on horse travois in about fifteen minutes.

What games did Slow play?

He ran races, sometimes in the hottest part of the day. Slow was fast. He and his friends would also spin tops. For another game someone would toss a hoop covered with net in the air, and other kids would try to throw spears through it. In the winter they would go sledding on a sled that had buffalo-rib runners.

Many of the children's games were rough. In one, everyone shot blunt arrows at a boy who had to use a shield and move fast to keep from being hit. They also had wrestling matches and played team sports. In one sport, the teams threw mud balls or hot coals at each other with willow sticks. The first team to run away lost. In "Throwing-Them-Off-Their-Horses," two teams of boys rode toward each other and tried to knock each other off their ponies. There was no crying allowed, of course.

Do your parents want you to play these games?

Probably not. These games helped Slow and his friends become warriors and hunters. They learned to hit a moving target and not to be hit when someone shot at them. They learned to be fast and tough. They had to be. Lakota toddlers slept at night with their moccasins on, in case an enemy tribe attacked and they had to run away.

Did Slow go to school?

Not in a school building, but he still had a lot to learn and many grown-ups to teach him. Slow's father and his uncles, especially Four Horns, were his teachers. Slow learned the stories of his people.

He heard about warriors's deeds and successful hunts and about how the Great Mysterious created the world. He heard the story of White Buffalo Woman, who had appeared to two warriors in a vision. She gave the Lakota the peace pipe and taught them to go on vision quests and perform the Sun Dance.

What did Slow learn besides stories?

He had to learn the same things his games taught him: how to be a hunter and a warrior and a good Lakota.

When Slow was still a toddler, his uncle or father made him a small bow and some arrows and taught him to use them. At three or four years old, Slow may have shot small animals for his mother to cook.

Slow's father taught him to recognize animals from their tracks. If he followed a horse's tracks, he could tell if the horse was male or female from where its pee landed as it walked. That was important. *Mares* (female horses) carried women, so a mare's tracks couldn't be a group of enemy warriors. Slow didn't have to learn to read words, but he had to read the world all around him.

Slow learned everything about horses. Before he could walk, he was tied to a special baby saddle or rode with an adult. He could probably ride alone by three, climbing up a horse's leg to mount. Like other little boys, Slow took care of the family's horses, bringing them to water every morning and leading them to fresh grass. Most boys had their own pony when they were eight, or even younger if their family could afford to give them one.

Did Slow like having a pony?

Of course. Boys rode their ponies and imagined being great warriors and hunters. By the time they were ten or twelve years old, many of them rode better than most people ever will. They learned to ride with no hands because they needed their hands free to shoot. They could hang sideways off their horses attached by the horses' bridles and their own legs, so that the horses' bodies made shields between them and their enemies. They also talked to their ponies and loved them, as Slow loved his favorite warhorse, Lump-on-Its-Jaw, when he was a grown-up warrior.

How old was Slow when he killed his first buffalo?

Ten. It was a small one, which was okay because he was pretty small to be a hunter. He said, much later, "When I was ten years old, I was famous as a hunter. My specialty was buffalo calves. I gave the calves that I killed to the poor that had no horses. I was considered a good man."

Was Sitting Bull bragging?

Yes. It was good to brag about things you'd done in a hunt or in a battle—in fact, you were expected to. And one of the things people could brag about was how much they gave away. Generosity was as important as bravery to the Lakota. When a family was celebrating a wedding or the birth of a child, they would give away horses (if they had any extra).

Why was killing a buffalo such a big deal?

Being able to hunt was one of the things that made a boy into a man. Men hunted the buffalo, and women made the buffalo into everything the family needed.

What could the Lakota make from a buffalo?

Practically everything.

❝Every part of their [the buffaloes'] flesh is converted into food. The skins are worn by the Indians and are used as coverings for their tipis and beds. The horns are shaped into spoons; their bones are used for war clubs and scrapers; their sinews are used for strings and backs to their bows and for thread to string their beads and sew their dresses. The feet of the animals are boiled, with their hooves, for glue. The hair from the head is twisted and braided into halters and the tail is used for a fly brush.❞

—**George Catlin,** writing about the Plains peoples in the 1830s

How important were the buffalo to the Lakota?

They planned their whole year around following the buffalo herds. The buffalo kept moving to eat fresh grass, and the Lakota kept moving to eat fresh buffalo (except in winter when they mostly ate the dried buffalo they had stored up). In the summer they gathered to have meetings and dances and a big hunt.

In a raid against another tribe, everyone knew that the leader would suggest an attack plan and that the young men might not listen. That's life. In a buffalo hunt, however, the *akicita*, or Indian police, stopped anyone from riding out ahead and frightening the herd. A warrior could risk his own life but not the well-being of the whole group.

How big is a buffalo?

Enormous. A *bull*, or male, buffalo stands about seven feet high at its shoulder—as high as a doorway in a house—and about fifteen feet from nose to rear end. It weighs about 2500 pounds. You really can't move a sitting bull.

How big were the buffalo herds?

In 1831 there were about forty or fifty million buffalo roaming around the plains. In 1862 someone saw a herd five or six miles wide gallop by for over an hour. Sometimes the plains looked like they had live buffalo wall-to-wall carpeting, except that there were no walls, just distant horizons, and the carpeting was moving fast.

What was a vision quest?

The Lakota believed that everything in nature—animals, thunder, trees, winds—had an invisible spirit. A Lakota man needed to find out about those spirits, to see which ones would speak to him. Those that spoke would help him find strength when he needed it.

When did Slow go on his vision quest?

Sometime after he killed his first buffalo, because the vision quest was for boys who were ready to become men.

What happened when Slow went on his vision quest?

A holy man helped Slow get ready. Slow went to the *sweat lodge*. (It's like a sauna. Water is poured on hot rocks to make steam and you sweat like crazy.) Slow stayed there a long time and chanted prayers. Then, after his body and his insides and even his thoughts were cleansed, he went off by himself, not eating or sleeping.

He smoked the sacred pipe and prayed that a spirit would speak to him, promising to guard him and telling him if there were things he shouldn't eat or places he shouldn't go. It might tell him how to paint himself when he went to war and what special objects (stones, feathers, pieces of animal fur) to carry to protect himself. Then he'd go back, and the holy man would help him understand his vision. We can't know what Slow heard, because these visions were private.

Did animals speak to people at other times?

They did to some people, and Slow was one of them. When he was about twelve, a yellow bird woke him from a nap and told him a grizzly bear was coming. Slow lay very still until the bear went away. At other times animals asked Slow for help. Once a wounded wolf asked the boy to take the arrows out of him. Many boys heard animals speak during their vision quests, but not at other times. Being able to understand animals was a special gift, and it wasn't private. Animals spoke to Slow's father, too.

Did Slow and his father really understand animals?

The Lakota believed they did. They also believed that Sitting Bull sometimes knew what would happen in the future. They believed he had powers that were *wakan*, which means mysterious, strange, special, worthy of wonder—and hard to understand. (So it's okay if they're hard for us to understand.)

When people have to say *wakan* in English, they sometimes say "holy," but *wakan* means more. Animals that people could eat were *wakan* because they helped people live. The border between Canada and the United States was the "*wakan* line." No one could see it, but white people from one side weren't allowed to go to the other side. White people were *wakan* because they were so strange.

And *everything* was part of Wakantanka—the Great Mysterious who had created the world.

Can we believe any of this if we're not Lakota?

Maybe. Some scientists say these visions don't mean anything. Other scientists say we can learn from our dreams. The Lakota believed that visions were messages from Wakantanka, so they worked hard to understand them.

CHAPTER 3

Sitting Bulls and Running Horses

These buffalo were photographed by the famous Edward S. Curtis.

What did a buffalo say to Slow's father?

One night, after a buffalo hunt, Returns-Again-to-Strike-the-Enemy and some other men were sitting around a buffalo chip fire. When they heard a noise, they thought it might be the Crow Indians, their old enemies. But it wasn't. It was a huge bull buffalo, a *tatanka*, and it came right up near them making buffalo noises. Everyone could hear it, but only Returns-Again could understand what the buffalo was saying. He understood four names: Sitting Bull, Jumping Bull, Bull-Standing-with-Cow, and Lone Bull. Since only Returns-Again could understand the buffalo, the names were his to use. After that he called himself Sitting Bull, until he gave the name to his son.

What did Slow do to earn his new name?

He did something brave in a battle.

When Slow was fourteen, he joined a war party against the Crow. As far as anyone knows, this was his first raid, and no one invited him to join it. Everyone in the war party of twenty or thirty men was surprised when the boy turned up the first evening. "We are going, too," Slow announced, meaning himself and his horse. "You have a good running horse," his father said. "Try to do something brave."

Slow painted himself and his gray horse with war paint and carried a special stick his father had given him. Then everyone hid, waiting for the "go ahead" signal from the warrior who had planned the raid. But instead of waiting, Slow went charging out by himself, and everyone went charging after Slow. There were many Lakota, so the Crow ran away, but Slow went after them. When he caught up with one Crow, the man turned to fight. He aimed an arrow toward Slow, but the boy hit the Crow on the arm with his stick, shouting, "*On-hey!* I, Slow, have conquered him!" The rest of the war party was right behind him, and they killed that Crow and some others. But Slow had touched a live enemy. That was the highest war honor possible—even braver than killing someone.

What did the war party do after the raid?

A painted shield cover from around 1870

They returned home singing. Then they had a feast and told stories of the battle. Slow's father gave away horses in celebration of his son's brave act. He gave Slow a shield, which he always used after that. Slow now had the right to wear a white eagle feather to war. And Slow's father gave his name to his son. The father would now be named Jumping Bull.

And the new Sitting Bull would be Sitting Bull for the rest of his life. In Lakota: Tatan'ka Iyota'ke.

What kind of war is this anyway?

Plains Indians' fighting sometimes sounds like a sport, because it had rules and warriors kept score. But it was serious. And people did get killed.

Why was hitting someone with a stick a bigger honor than killing him?

Warriors fought to show their courage. Touching a live enemy was brave. Shooting someone from far away was "just killing." It wasn't brave and it wasn't interesting. The warrior who touched an enemy Indian first said he had "counted first coup." Even if someone else killed that enemy, the man who touched him first got to keep his scalp, like a soldier's medal of honor.

Counting a coup was like getting a point in a very extreme sport. Other honors were stealing horses, taking away a live enemy's weapon, rescuing a friend on the battlefield, and killing someone in hand-to-hand combat.

Once, some warriors peed on an enemy who had fallen asleep guarding the horses. Then they stole the horses. Leaving the man alive, wet, and without horses was braver (and funnier) than killing him.

Why did warriors kill babies?

Since war was about honor and courage, you might think that Plains Indians would kill only warriors. In real life, it didn't work that way. Some warriors would do anything to hurt and insult their enemies, so they would kill or kidnap the people their enemies were trying to protect—their families.

No tribe could let too many warriors get killed because the tribe had to feed all its families. So a battle could end when enough people had done something brave or when too many people had been hurt.

Did the Lakota really scalp people?

A Sioux scalp ornament

Yes, although sometimes they chopped them up instead. The Plains Indians scalped people because hair is special: It keeps growing as long as a person lives. It seemed to the Lakota that hair must be connected to a person's spirit. If you scalped an enemy, then you took his spirit, and he couldn't travel to the world people go to after they're dead.

That's why they wouldn't scalp and cut up the same person. The Plains Indians believed that you go to the next world in the shape you leave this one. If they chopped up a warrior, then he went to the next world chopped up. A scalped person couldn't go to the next world at all.

That's also why Plains warriors would risk their lives to bring dead friends off the battlefield. They wanted to make sure their friends went to the next world in one piece.

Whites said scalping was "savage" and disgusting, but white fur trappers, cowboys, and even soldiers in the United States Army scalped Indians and cut them up. In some states, like Pennsylvania, the government had paid a *bounty*, or reward, for Indian scalps.

What weapons did Lakota warriors use?

A coup stick. A warrior often marked his coups on his coup stick.

A bow and arrows. War arrows had barbed tips, like fishhooks, so that the only way to remove one was to push it all the way through. They couldn't be pulled out.

A tomahawk (also called a war club). An egg-shaped stone attached with rawhide strips to a strong handle. A tomahawk was good for cracking skulls.

A hatchet. A sort of cross between a hammer and an ax, with a metal head.

A gun (very old-fashioned guns—until about 1870, a bow and arrow was easier to aim and faster to reload).

A shield. Shields were made of layers of buffalo rawhide. They were strong enough to stop arrows and even bullets, if the bullets weren't coming straight at them. A shield had powerful symbols on it, for another kind of protection.

A knife.

A whip.

A lance.

Would a warrior carry all these weapons?

Of course not. Even the best Plains warrior had only two hands. People fought at different times with different weapons or would use their favorite. As a young man, Sitting Bull was very good at fighting with his lance. It had blue and white beads and an eagle feather on it—and an eight-inch-long iron blade for spearing people and horses.

Besides, things go wrong with weapons. In 1876 one warrior owned a rifle (but had no bullets for it) and a six-shooter (but had loaned it to a cousin). He went to war with a bow and arrows that the cousin had borrowed from someone else.

How did warriors get ready for battle?

They painted themselves with war paint. Some people have said that war paint was to scare the enemy. Really it was more for the warrior himself. The warrior put his life in order and made himself and his spirit ready to fight, just as many modern soldiers (and sports teams) pray or have special ceremonies before a battle (or important game). The Lakota warrior painted himself with stripes, zigzags, dots, or other designs. He painted his horse, too. He might paint a horseshoe for every horse-stealing raid he'd been on. Red handprints painted on a horse showed how many scalps the warrior had taken. In the same way, fighter pilots in World War II marked their planes with each "hit."

Of course, it wasn't so bad if the war paint did scare the enemy. Lakota warriors sometimes went into battle growling like grizzly bears or yipping and yelling. It made them feel brave *and* it frightened the enemy. It also called attention to their brave actions.

Did Indian warriors wear armor?

War clothes helped keep warriors from attacking people on their own side. War clothes also showed what honors a warrior had earned. Lakota warriors wore a white feather for each coup they had made and a red feather for each time they had been hurt. Only a few men could wear the big feathered war bonnets you see in movies and museums. Sitting Bull could.

Often warriors wore fine clothes, decorated with painted designs, beads, porcupine quills, or hair (of enemies or from friends, to protect them). As one old Lakota man explained, warrior clothes made a man feel braver, and if he was going to be killed he wanted to look good.

Sometimes warriors wore very little besides their loincloth and war paint. They wore their fancy warrior clothes to the feasts before a fight (like military dress uniforms) and wore simple clothes into battle. Sitting Bull dressed very simply. He didn't have to dress up. Everyone knew who he was.

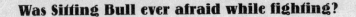

We can't know for sure. Good warriors learn not to show fear. A Lakota who was afraid would try not to show it. Children grew up hearing warriors brag of their war deeds, and the children imitated them in their games. They were very well trained before they had to fight.

Lakota children had to get over being afraid of dead bodies, so after a battle a warrior would drag a dead enemy (or pieces of the enemy) through the village. Boys were supposed to hit the body with rocks or shoot it with arrows. When Slow was ten, a warrior dared the boys to touch pieces of a Crow warrior, and Slow went first. Later, as Sitting Bull, he showed his bravery in many battles.

Still, the Lakota knew that some days were just unlucky. A man could leave a battle *before* it began if his spirit helper told him to. No one would laugh at him or call him a coward. If many people in a war party felt unlucky, they'd just call the whole thing off.

Why did Indians fight each other?

The Native peoples were different nations. Some were allies and some were enemies, just like different countries. And, like enemy countries, they fought to get more land. There was no word in their languages for "Indians." They were Lakota or Crow or Navajo. Even on the Plains, their languages were so different that people spoke in sign language.

Later, after all the Native peoples had been conquered by whites, some tribes began to talk about themselves as Indians or as "red" people. Even though they were from different nations, they could see ways they were alike.

If green creatures from Mars conquered our whole world, earthlings would probably begin to see more similarities than differences among ourselves, too.

WHAT COLOR WAS "THE WHITE MAN"?

The Lakota word for whites was *Wasichus* (wah SEE chooz). But it doesn't mean "white" or "paleface." It means "the ones who take the fat." It describes the way white people acted, taking the best part of a buffalo and leaving the rest. The Lakota were describing greed, not skin color.

Most of the Wasichus the Indians saw were white—first the French, then the English, and then all the many European-Americans who went West—but there were black soldiers and settlers, too, and the Lakota saw them. People from China built the railroads. Sitting Bull's people may not have seen them, but other tribes did.

White men were the presidents and the generals, but the fight over who would live on this continent wasn't just a struggle between "whites" and "reds." All the men and women who came to this continent are part of this story.

Why did the Plains Indians like to fight? Why didn't they want peace?

It's hard for us to understand a warrior culture. A lot of countries would rather be at peace, even if they have to fight a war. Teachers and parents say, "Don't hit. Use your words." But the Lakota liked war, especially with enemy tribes. They fought with amazing skill and bravery. On a good day, no one on their side got killed. It was exciting to them.

All people "count coups" in some way. Modern kids and adults can count coups with good grades, new toys, designer clothes, sports trophies, or money. We all want to succeed at something that shows off our skills and makes us look good. That's what the Lakota were doing.

They were also annoying the other tribes. When Sitting Bull was born, the Teton Lakota hadn't been in the Plains very long and they had stepped on a lot of toes getting there.

❝Better to die on the battlefield than to grow old.**❞**

—Lakota saying

Hadn't the Plains Indians lived there for ages, riding horses and hunting the buffalo?

No, they hadn't been there very long at all. In the early 1700s, Sitting Bull's people were still hunting and farming in Minnesota, many miles east of where he was born. They were forest Indians, not Plains Indians. But in the 1700s, some of the forest tribes got guns from French traders. These tribes forced the Lakota to move west, very slowly, over the next eighty years. The Lakota's way of life changed as they became better and better hunters and discovered the richness of the wild game on the Plains. While the Santee settled down farther east and continued to farm, the Teton Lakota became full-time buffalo hunters.

But hunting buffalo on foot is hard. Buffalo run faster than people do. The Lakota had to get everyone together and try to scare buffalo off a cliff or shoot them one at a time. When they moved from place to place, they had to carry everything or have dogs drag their belongings behind them on little travois. Sometimes old or sick relatives had to be left behind—until they got horses.

❝My horse be swift in flight
Even like a bird:
My horse be swift in flight,
Bear me now in safety
Far from the enemy's arrows,
And you shall be rewarded
With streamers and ribbons red. **❞**
—A Lakota warrior's song to his horse

Where did Indians get horses?

Sioux on their sturdy horses

The wild horses of North America became extinct at the end of the last ice age, about fifteen thousand years ago—the same time the woolly mammoths

40

and saber-toothed tigers died out. Then the Spanish came to the "New World" (which was the Indians' old world) in the 1520s. They settled in what is now Mexico, bringing their horses with them. After a while, some horses got loose or were stolen. With no natural enemies, the horses multiplied quickly. Many of the Indian nations loved them. The Indians called them "big dogs" and "sacred (*wakan*) dogs."

What were horses good for?

Horses made it possible to move as fast as a charging buffalo. The Plains Indians could hunt better and have buffalo hides to trade for metal arrowheads and cloth. Warriors would have specially trained warhorses—in an emergency a man could grab a warhorse's tail and it would pull him out of the fight.

Horses could pull more than dogs could. Tipis could be bigger, and Grandma and sick people could have a ride. Families could be bigger. People didn't have to worry so much about starving during the winter. After they got horses, there were more Lakota people.

What else happened to the Lakota after they got horses?

They got guns from white traders, too. Then they were the biggest, toughest tribe anywhere. They took over the territories of other tribes. From the end of the 1700s until the middle of the 1800s, no one could beat the Teton Lakota.

What is strange and sad is that guns traded by whites to Indians had made the Lakota leave their old land in Minnesota and travel west. Horses and guns from whites helped the Lakota make themselves the strongest tribe in the Plains. Then the whites moved west and destroyed the life that horses and guns had created.

CHAPTER 4

Chief Sitting Bull

From Sitting Bull's autobiography

How do we know that Sitting Bull became a great warrior?

He rode into fights yelling, "Sitting Bull, I am he!" to scare his enemies. By the time Sitting Bull was in his twenties, even older men would ride into battle shouting, "We are Sitting Bull's boys!" It was a battle cry, as good as a grizzly bear roar for spooking the Crow.

SITTING BULL'S AUTOBIOGRAPHY

Sitting Bull painted pictures of his many coups in a notebook. He counted forty-one coups in the 1850s and 1860s. In 1870 someone stole the notebook from him and sold it to a doctor at a fort.

What did warriors do besides fight?

One thing they did was join war societies. In 1852, when he was in his early twenties, Sitting Bull was elected to the Strong Hearts and Kit Fox Societies. Only brave warriors were asked to join, so it was a big honor.

Was a warrior society like a military unit?

No, because the warrior societies didn't actually fight together. A man fought with his family or friends or with whoever he thought was a good war leader. Men in the warrior societies gathered to eat, talk, sing, and advise the chiefs and headmen of the band.

Some of them would also be chosen to be the *akicita* (the Indian police), who protected the village at night and during hunts, and enforced important rules. If a group of young men wanted to leave a buffalo hunt to go horse stealing, then the *akicita* would try to stop them. If the young men went anyway, the *akicita* could burn down their tipis.

Were warriors supposed to get married?

A man who was good at hunting and war was supposed to marry a wife or two. Sitting Bull got married in about 1852, when he was about twenty-one, to a woman named Light Hair. She died giving birth in their first year together. We don't know much about their marriage.

The Lakota thought it made sense for a man to marry more than one wife if he could afford to. There were more women than men because so many men were killed in battles, and everyone needed to be part of a family. Also, the women had so much to do that it was good to have someone to share the work. A good Lakota man married and had children and adopted people and took care of his relatives.

Did Sitting Bull ever get hurt in battle?

Sitting Bull had a gift for coming out of battles without a scratch. But he did get hurt sometimes. In 1856 a Crow chief shot Sitting Bull in the foot. Sitting Bull limped for the rest of his life, but he killed and scalped that chief. Being hard to hurt in battle and killing a chief showed that his power was strong.

Didn't Sitting Bull do anything but fight and steal horses?

Yes. He had fast horses and was often at the front in a buffalo hunt. He would kill three or four buffalo and give them to needy families. He told jokes and made up songs. Animals and spirits spoke to him, and he could foretell the future. And he performed many ceremonies. One was the Sun Dance.

What was the Sun Dance?

In the summer, the Hunkpapa got together. Everyone decided where to go for the big buffalo hunt. And most summers people held the Sun Dance. It was the most *wakan* ceremony of all those taught to the Lakota by White Buffalo Woman.

In the summer of 1856, Sitting Bull performed the Sun Dance for the first time. Young women cut down a cottonwood tree and chopped the branches off it. Young men planted the tree in the middle of a circle of sturdy posts set deep in the ground. Then they set out a decorated buffalo skull at its base. The ceremonies preparing for the Sun Dance went on for days before the actual dance.

There were different ways of doing the Sun Dance. Some men just danced, staring at the sun, not eating or sleeping. Some cut bits of flesh out of their arms before they danced. Some danced with wooden skewers inserted beneath the flesh of their chests or backs. The skewers either had buffalo skulls hanging from them or were attached by a cord to the tree at the center of the brushwood circle.

After a day or two, the skewers would tear through the dancers' flesh or the holy men would cut them out. Dancers would fall to the ground, exhausted, having had powerful visions for the tribe. When a boy went on his vision quest, it was for himself. The Sun Dance was for all his people. Dancers chanted, "Wakantanka, have mercy on me, let the tribe live long and let us have lots of buffalo. Let no one get sick so the tribe will increase." The Sun Dance was like a prayer said with the whole body.

Was this weird?

> **WHAT DOES IT MEAN?**
> **Fortitude** is the ability to bear pain or troubles bravely.

Not as weird as it might sound at first. *Fortitude* was important to the Lakota. Think of the games they played when they were children. Also, most religions have times of fasting or sacrifice. In cultures around the world, people are pierced, scarred, or tattooed when they become adults. And no one had to do the Sun Dance if they didn't want to.

When did Sitting Bull become a chief?

The Strong Hearts made Sitting Bull a chief in 1857, when he was twenty-six.

What did it mean to be a chief?

Not what most people think. A chief wasn't like a king or even like a president. He couldn't tell people what to do. Well, he could try, but no one had to listen to him. The Lakota didn't like to be bossed around.

A chief had to be a good leader. If he gave good advice, then people would listen to him. If he gave bad advice, then they wouldn't listen. They might even go join another Hunkpapa hunting band, one with better chiefs.

A chief had to be brave, wise, and patient. A chief who lost his temper was no help to anyone. He had to have proved his fortitude, as Sitting Bull did at the Sun Dance. And he had to be generous. A chief's wife should have a big cooking pot, the Lakota said. Keeping people fed and safe was the job of the chiefs (there was more than one) and of the headmen.

Was Sitting Bull a good chief?

Yes. A good chief was one who had a big family and many lodges camped around him. Years later an old man said that Sitting Bull "fed the whole nation." Sitting Bull was a great warrior and a holy man, but he was also very good at feeding people.

Why is it important to know what chiefs could and couldn't do?

Later on, the U.S. government wanted someone who could speak for all the Lakota and sign a treaty for them. Government officials couldn't believe that every time they wanted to make a treaty they had to talk to the whole tribe. What a pain!

And it's good to understand that the Lakota believed that every person got to make up his or her own mind about things.

Why did Sitting Bull adopt an enemy boy?

About the same time that Sitting Bull became a chief, he adopted his sister's younger son, One Bull. He also taught her other boy, White Bull. That was the kind of thing an uncle was supposed to do. Adopting an enemy boy was not the sort of thing everyone was supposed to do.

This is how it happened. Sitting Bull and three friends went out on a war party against a tribe called the Assiniboin. They could find only one Assiniboin lodge, with a mother, a father, a baby and a young boy in it. Assiniboin were enemies, so they killed the parents and the baby. But the older boy, who was about eleven, didn't run away or cry. He tried to shoot the Hunkpapa. They were going to kill him, but he called Sitting Bull "older brother." Sitting Bull said, "Don't shoot him. This boy is too brave to die. I have no brother. I take this one for my brother. Let him live."

What did the other warriors think?

They thought this was a lousy idea. Warriors would often take enemy babies or women to live with them—or white women and children—to increase their numbers. A boy old enough to shoot at them was another story. He was dangerous. But Sitting Bull was someone people listened to, and the rest of the band agreed to take the boy in. Then Sitting Bull adopted him. He gave a special feast. He and the boy promised that they would always be loyal to each other. Sitting Bull gave away horses in celebration. He gained honor for making this boy his brother, and he made his family bigger.

AMERICAN VOICES

❝ All are my relatives. ❞
—Lakota prayer

How would a chief look out for others?

Sitting Bull risked his life to rescue a girl's favorite horse. It had been left behind when the band crossed a river and the river had flooded overnight. People said it was too dangerous to get the horse. But Sitting Bull swam across the river. "Grandchild," he said to the horse, "I have been sent to come to your rescue. Do not run away from me. Somebody is waiting for you on the other side." Then he rode the horse back across the rushing river.

How did Sitting Bull's father die?

One day in 1859 the Hunkpapa were moving camp when fifty Crow warriors attacked them. Sitting Bull's father had lived more than sixty winters. He was too old to fight. But Jumping Bull had a bad toothache. Old age and a toothache were not a good way for a warrior to die. Fighting the Crow, on the other hand, was a very good way to die, so he joined the fight and was killed. The Hunkpapa chased Jumping Bull's killer and called for Sitting Bull, who struck the Crow with his lance. The Hunkpapa also captured some Crow women, intending to kill them in revenge for Jumping Bull's death. Sitting Bull said, "Take care of them, and let them live. My father was a man, and death is his."

How did the Hunkpapa mourn Jumping Bull?

Sitting Bull would have entered camp wailing. He would have cut his warhorse's tail or cut his own braids off. A holy man would have painted Jumping Bull's face in his war paint and dressed him in his best clothes. Plains Indians didn't bury dead people, because wild animals would dig them up again. Instead they wrapped Jumping Bull in a buffalo robe and put him on a platform raised above the ground on poles. Underneath they put the body of his favorite horse, so that Jumping Bull's spirit could ride the spirit horse to the next world. There, somewhere in the stars, he would be with his ancestors and hunt the buffalo.

Sitting Bull gave his father's name to his adopted brother.

Since Sitting Bull was so good at fighting enemy Indians, was he good at fighting the whites?

He never did as a young man, as far as we know. At least he didn't fight soldiers. Sitting Bull was in his middle thirties before the whites became a problem for the Hunkpapa.

CHAPTER 5

The Hairy Men and the Indians

An etching of Lewis and Clark holding a council with the Indians

Were there white people around when Sitting Bull was growing up?

Yes, but not many of them. Before Sitting Bull was born, most of the white people the Plains people saw were fur trappers and traders. Sometimes a missionary would come to try to convert the Indians to Christianity.

Then, in 1803, the United States bought the Louisiana Territory from France. President Jefferson sent Meriwether Lewis and William Clark to check it out. How big was it? Could they get all the way to the Pacific Ocean by boat? What were the Indians like? One of their jobs was to tell all the Indians that the land now belonged to the United States and that the Indians had a new "Grandfather" in Washington, D.C.

In 1806 Lewis and Clark reported back about rivers and animals, new plants and minerals, and the tallest mountains either of them had ever seen—the Rocky Mountains. They also reported that they had met up with some Indians called Sioux, who wanted to know what Lewis and Clark thought they were doing there.

More traders went west, as well as trappers and hunters. But when Sitting Bull was born, there were still not very many whites near the Lakota's territory.

What did the Lakota think of the whites?

They thought the whites were strange. Whites were so pale that they looked sick and so hairy that the Indians sometimes called them "dog faces" or "hairy men." The Indians didn't have much hair on their bodies and they thought body hair was gross. White people smelled bad to the Lakota—like porcupines. But the Lakota trusted some of the traders and got along pretty well with them.

Was trade a good thing for the Plains peoples?

Traders brought good and bad things to the Lakota. The Lakota liked guns, woven cloth, metal pots, metal knives, and beads. But the traders cut down trees to build trading posts. They brought terrible diseases with them. Smallpox and measles were dangerous to whites, but they almost always killed Indians. (Sitting Bull survived having smallpox.) The traders also brought "trader's whiskey" made of cheap alcohol, red pepper, and chewing tobacco. For many Indians alcohol was (and is) a dangerous drug. Some Indians would kill hundreds of buffalo to trade for whiskey.

When did the relationship between Plains Indians and whites start to change?

About the time Sitting Bull killed his first buffalo, in 1841, but it would be many years before the Hunkpapa would feel the change. When the farmlands of California and the Oregon territory were opened up for settlement, the people of the United States began to move west, but they still didn't come too near the Hunkpapa's hunting grounds.

How many people traveled west?

The first covered wagons rolled west along the Oregon Trail in 1842, but in 1843 only about nine hundred people traveled it. The Indians could live with that. Then, in 1848, gold was discovered in California. Fifty-five thousand people went west in 1850, right through

> **AMERICAN VOICES**
>
> 66 We did not think of the great open plains, the beautiful rolling hills, and tangled growths as 'wild.' Only to the white man was nature a 'wilderness' and only to him was the land 'infested' with 'wild' animals and 'savage' people. To us it was tame. 99
>
> —Luther Standing Bear

Oglala Lakota hunting grounds. An Oglala chief stared at this heavy traffic and asked a pioneer if there were still any whites back east.

The pioneers were cutting a deep path across the land. (In some places you can still see the ruts their wagon wheels made.) There still wasn't a lot of trouble between whites and Plains peoples. The pioneers were more likely to die of sickness, starvation, runaway horses, or drowning than they were from Indian attacks. But some whites and Indians killed one another, and it made the whites nervous. By the late 1840s, the United States Army built forts along the trail to protect the pioneers, and the Indians didn't like it.

What did the whites think of the Indians?

Different things. Some were disgusted by people who didn't wear enough clothes. Some said that the Indians were kind to their children and sure could ride horses well.

Some were afraid. Back in the 1600s, when the United States was still an English colony, people were already telling stories about Indians scalping people or torturing them. Only some of the stories were true. Early settlers had also learned from Indians how to make *pemmican* and grow corn, but—just like now—the good news usually isn't what shows up in newspaper headlines.

How did a lost cow lead to warfare between the Lakota and whites?

In August 1854 a cow wandered into a Brulé Lakota camp near Fort Laramie. A visiting Miniconjou Lakota shot it and gave a feast. A young lieutenant, John Grattan, was stationed at the fort. The trouble was, young U.S. military officers, like young Lakota warriors,

WHAT DOES IT MEAN?

To make **pemmican**, lean meat was dried, pounded fine, and mixed with melted fat. It could be stored for a long time without spoiling.

wanted to prove they were brave and tough. This one showed up at the Brulé camp with twenty-nine *cavalrymen*, two cannons, and an interpreter who got drunk on the way there.

Brulé camp as it appeared in 1891

WHAT DOES IT MEAN?

Cavalrymen are soldiers who fight on horseback.

The interpreter told Chief Conquering Bear that they had come to kill the Indians, cut them into little pieces, and eat their hearts. Conquering Bear offered to pay for the cow, but he couldn't tell Grattan who had shot it. The Lakota believe that they must always protect guests, and this guest was going to be in big trouble. Grattan ordered his troops to shoot the chief. Then the warriors killed Grattan and all his men. Grattan had twenty-four arrows in him. Conquering Bear survived. This was the first time Plains Indians had fought American soldiers, and they hadn't even started the fight, but newspaper headlines said: "Avenge the Grattan Massacre!"

Did the army get revenge?

Yes, they always did. In the fall of 1855, Colonel William S. Harney invaded a Brulé Lakota camp. The chief tried to surrender, but Harney's troops killed eighty-seven people and destroyed the camp.

Newswalkers, who carried news from camp to camp, would have carried this story to the Hunkpapa. This sort of thing had never happened to them before. The Lakota made war and killed families, but they didn't leave a whole village without food and shelter right before the winter. They called Harney "Mad Bear." This may have been Sitting Bull's introduction to white warfare.

Could whites and Lakota ever have lived in peace?

No. White people had been "moving west" since they sailed from Europe. The English had been getting rid of Indians since about 1600. They had three ways to do this—kill them, move them to parts of the land the whites didn't want, or send them to special land set aside for them—reservations— where they could be taught to live like white people.

Why did whites in the United States and Canada think it was okay to take Indian lands?

The tribes were always fighting about the boundaries of their territories, whites said. If the tribes didn't know who owned what, why should the whites pay any attention? Other whites said the Indians just moved across the land "like animals" and so they didn't have any right to it at all.

Whites thought people owned land. Native peoples did not. That would be like saying you owned the sky or the wind. Whites believed God had given them the land, and Indians believed Wakantanka had given it to them. These different beliefs led to serious problems.

AMERICAN VOICES

❝ As I passed over the very best cornlands on earth and saw their owners sitting around the door of their lodges at the height of the planting season, I could not help saying, 'These people must die out. God has given this earth to those who will tame and cultivate it.' **❞**

—**Horace Greeley,** American newspaper writer and politician, 1859

❝ Hear me, people, we have now to deal with another race. Strangely enough they have a mind to plough the soil and the love of ownership is a disease with them. They claim this mother of ours, the earth, for their own; they deface her with their buildings and their refuse [garbage]. **❞**

—**Sitting Bull,** 1877

So, were the pioneers bad people?

Some of the people who went west did terrible things. They cheated and killed Indians and one another. But most people went west for the same reasons they had come to America in the first place, and they didn't mean to do anything wrong.

People came because there was land here. They came because they'd be killed in their own countries for being the wrong religion or having the wrong political

AMERICAN VOICES

❝ We cross the prairies as of old
The Pilgrims crossed the sea,
To make the West,
as they, the East,
The homestead of the free. ❞
— From a song, "The Kansas Emigrant"

beliefs. They came because they were starving. (Around the time Sitting Bull counted his first coup, thousands of people came to America from Ireland because the potato crops had failed and they had nothing to eat.) Escaping and freed slaves went west to finally have their own houses and towns.

No one had ever seen a land as big and empty and free as the American West.

On the other hand, once Americans and the British made a treaty over who owned Canada, the U.S. government didn't think it was okay to take land away from white people in Canada. Just from Indians.

What were the American pioneers doing in the 1860s?

They were traveling west in greater and greater numbers, and worrying—with more and more reason—about Indian attacks. They were also settling on the Plains for the first time. An 1862 law called the Homestead Act promised 160 acres of land to anyone who would live on the land and farm it for five years. The Hunkpapa sent a message to the men they traded with. It said, "We wish you to stop the whites from travelling through our country, and if you do not stop them, we will." The Lakota raided wagon trains, settlements, and forts.

What was so great about the Great Plains?

For a long time, nothing. Old maps call the area the "Great American Desert." White farmers couldn't even farm it until a steel plow was invented in the 1850s. The sod, hundreds of years of tangled grass roots and dirt, made the ground so hard that settlers cut bricks and built houses out of it. The temperature could be 40 below zero in the winter and 110 degrees in the summer. But it wasn't really a desert with sand and cactuses. It was prairie, grassy land that was sometimes hilly and sometimes flat. As America's population grew and more people wanted land, homesteaders settled in places that once seemed only a good way to get somewhere else.

What was the biggest Indian uprising in U.S. history?

The Minnesota uprising of 1862.

In 1851 the Santee signed a treaty. They promised to leave the forts and settlers alone. The treaty promised the tribe money and food in exchange for its land. So by 1862 many Santee lived on reservations, but they were starving. The United States was too busy fighting the Civil War to feed them.

U.S. POPULATION

1790 (first census): 3.9 million people

1831 (the year of Sitting Bull's birth): 13 million people

1890: (the year of Sitting Bull's death): 63 million people

One Sunday in August 1862, a group of Santee raided the *agencies*, which were full of food for the soldiers. At one agency the Santee were laughed at and insulted. A white trader told them, "Go and eat grass."

In response, Indian war parties spread out for a hundred miles in all directions, killing and chopping up settlers, including teachers, missionaries, ministers, and children. The rude trader was

WHAT DOES IT MEAN?

On a reservation, the **agency** was the building where food and supplies were given out to the Indians.

found with his mouth full of grass. Bodies lined the streets of the towns. At least six hundred people were killed.

In books about pioneer life like *Little House on the Prairie* and *Caddie Woodlawn*, you can see how frightened the settlers were after the Minnesota uprising. The grown-ups in these books all whisper about it but won't tell the children what happened.

What did the United States do?

The courts sentenced more than three hundred Santee to death. Each trial took only five minutes. President Lincoln, who had been a lawyer before he was president, read the trial records. He said that people couldn't be hanged just for being Santee. They had to have taken part in the killings. It was still the largest public execution in American history. Thirty-eight Santee were hanged. At least a few others were killed by their families, who were furious and ashamed. Many went and joined other hunting bands. Almost half of the Santee who went back to the reservation starved to death that year.

Where was Sitting Bull during this time?

Probably raiding forts, but also raiding the Crow Indians for horses. The Hunkpapa were still not fighting the United States, and Sitting Bull didn't want to. He just wanted the whites to go away. When the Hunkpapa captured a white woman named Fanny Kelly, Sitting Bull sent her home. He said she looked homesick.

But Sitting Bull knew he'd soon have to fight the whites. The U.S. Army was hunting down the Santee. Whites had settled only two hundred miles away from Hunkpapa lands. The hairy men had come too close.

CHAPTER 6

Battles and Treaties

A painting of the 8th Minnesota Infantry at the Battle of Killdeer Mountain

What was Sitting Bull's first battle against white soldiers?

We can't know for sure, but one of the first was near what is now Killdeer Mountain, North Dakota. It was July 1864, and a U.S. army general named Alfred Sully was looking for Santee. He had already proved that he would settle for any Sioux he could find.

That day in July the Lakota were fighting two thousand soldiers and twelve cannons, and they remembered the battle because they lost it so badly. U.S. troops killed about a hundred Lakota and burned their village.

❝ My father has given me this nation;
In protecting them I have a hard time. ❞
—Sitting Bull's song during one of his first
battles against the army

Who won the 1860s wars between the Lakota and the whites?

No one. The end of the Civil War in 1865 freed up many soldiers to go fight the Indians—and many ex-soldiers and their families to settle the West.

At a place called Sand Creek, in 1864, a volunteer army (not U.S. soldiers) killed more than two hundred people in a peaceful Cheyenne village, even though Chief Black Kettle was flying an American flag and the white flag of surrender. An important government official had given Black Kettle the flag and told him he'd be safe if he showed it. After Sand Creek no more Southern Cheyenne tried to keep the peace.

But the biggest battle of this time was the fight of the Oglala against the Bozeman Trail.

AMERICAN VOICES

❝ The Great Spirit . . . raised me in this land and it belongs to me. The white man was raised over the waters, and his land is over there. There are now white men all around me. I have but a small spot of land left. The Great Spirit has told me to keep it. ❞
—**Red Cloud,** an Oglala Sioux chief

❝ [The Indians are] a set of miserable, dirty, lousy, blanketed, thieving, lying, sneaking, murdering, graceless, faithless, gut-eating skunks. ❞

—The Topeka, Kansas, newspaper *The Weekly Leader*

Freight train going through Bozeman Pass, 1939

What was the Bozeman Trail?

In 1863 a man named John Bozeman blazed a trail straight to the gold mines of Montana. The trail cut through the last of the big Oglala hunting grounds. Red Cloud and the Oglala Lakota said they'd fight, and they did, killing people traveling along the trail.

In 1866 the United States offered to buy the land from the Oglala, but before they even met, the United States was building forts along the Bozeman Trail. Red Cloud was furious. He and the great warrior Crazy Horse raided the forts and killed the travelers. People called the trail the "Bloody Bozeman."

Who were Red Cloud and Crazy Horse?

They were two of the most famous Oglala Lakota of the 1800s. Red Cloud believed he could make deals

Chief Red Cloud with peace pipe

with the whites. Crazy Horse, who was never photographed and seldom spoke, was a mystery even to the Oglala. He didn't make deals with anyone, but when he went into battle, the Oglala and the Miniconjou (his mother's people) and even the Cheyenne (who weren't Lakota) were glad to follow him.

What was the Fetterman Battle?

Captain William J. Fetterman was another John Grattan. He thought that his commanding officer was a wimp and that Indians couldn't fight. Fetterman bragged that with eighty men he could conquer the whole Sioux nation. In December 1866 Crazy Horse and a small band of warriors rode toward Fort Phil Kearny. When Fetterman and his eighty men came out to fight, the Lakota ran away, and Fetterman's troops followed. But this was an old trick. Suddenly hundreds of Lakota warriors surrounded them. The battle was over in twenty minutes.

This was the army's worst defeat in the West so far.

What did most Americans think when the Indians won a battle?

Many people wanted to kill all the Indians, but what they needed was safety for people going west. They wanted to keep the Indians away from the major trails and from the railroad being built to link the east and west coasts. They were willing to give up the Bozeman Trail and shut down the forts along it if they could get the Lakota peoples onto reservations. Red Cloud and many of the Oglala and Miniconjou and other Lakota were ready to sign a treaty.

What did the Fort Laramie Treaty of 1868 say?

The Lakota who signed the treaty agreed to move to the "Great Sioux Reservation." This was a huge piece of land that took up all of what is now South Dakota west of the Missouri River. People who lived on the reservation would receive food and clothing from the U.S. government while they learned to farm. They also would receive payments for many years. The treaty promised that the reservation land would belong to the Lakota "as long as the grass shall grow and the waters flow," unless three-quarters of the tribe's men agreed to sell it. The treaty also said that the Lakota had the right to hunt on the lands west of the reservation for as long as the buffalo roamed there. So people could come live on the reservation, or they could still be hunters.

Did this mean the Lakota had won?

Red Cloud thought so. The forts along the Bozeman Trail were closed, and Lakota warriors burned them to the ground. But the treaty wasn't as clear as the Lakota thought. One army officer at Fort Laramie said the Indians had no idea what they were signing. The treaty would allow the railroad to build tracks across the reservation. The Lakota didn't know that and wouldn't have agreed to it.

And whites didn't expect the buffalo to be around for much longer. In fact, they had hired people to kill the buffalo off as fast as possible. "For the sake of a lasting peace, let them kill, skin, and sell until the buffaloes are exterminated," General Philip Sheridan said. Without buffalo the Indians would have to live on the reservations.

AMERICAN VOICES

❝ We were born naked and have been taught to hunt and live on the game. You tell us we must learn to farm, live in one house, and take on your ways. Suppose the people living beyond the great sea should come and tell you that you must stop farming and kill your cattle, and take your houses and your lands, what would you do? Would you not fight them? ❞

—**Chief Gall,** a friend of Sitting Bull, to the treaty commissioners, 1868

Did Sitting Bull sign the treaty?

No. Sitting Bull never signed a single treaty with the United States.

Sitting Bull made fun of some Assiniboin who had moved to a reservation: "Look at me. See if I am poor, or my people either. The whites may get me at last, as you say, but I will have good times till then. You are fools to make yourself slaves to a piece of fat bacon, some hardtack, and a little sugar and coffee.

"I will not give away any part of my country," he said.

What happened after the signing of the Fort Laramie Treaty?

Between 1868 and 1869 most Teton Lakota—about 17,000 of them—moved to the reservation. Red Cloud realized later that he had not won a great victory after all. When he visited Washington, D.C., in 1870, he saw the military strength of the whites. "When we first had this land we were strong. Now we are melting like snow on a hillside, while you are growing like the spring grass," he said.

Sitting Bull, Gall, and most of the Hunkpapa refused to go to the reservation. So did Crazy Horse and some Lakota from different bands. About 3000 Lakota agreed with Crazy Horse: "We want to live as our fathers lived, and their fathers before them."

Why were Sitting Bull and his people in big trouble?

By 1868 there were reservations for all the Indian nations. "All who cling to their old hunting grounds are hostile and will remain so till killed off," said General William T. Sherman.

Some of the Indians who were on reservations were feeling hostile, too. For the peoples of the Plains, reservation life made no sense at all, especially for the young men who had been raised to be warriors. In August 1868 a war party of young Cheyenne men left their reservation and attacked some white settlers. The newspapers insisted that the army "do something" about the Indians—not just the Cheyenne but all the Indians still living off the reservations.

General Sherman and General Sheridan were famous Civil War generals, and they decided to fight the Indians as they had fought against the South: Instead of just killing warriors, they would destroy whole villages. (In the South, they had burned cities and destroyed farmers' fields.) Then, they believed, all the Indians would have to surrender. Sherman and Sheridan also decided to fight during the winter, when the Lakota and Cheyenne weren't expecting trouble.

What happened when Sherman and Sheridan started their new campaign?

The generals put a lieutenant colonel named George Armstrong Custer in charge of the campaign. At dawn Custer and the Seventh Cavalry attacked a Cheyenne village on the Washita River. It was the village of Black Kettle, half of whose people had been killed at Sand Creek. Custer and the Seventh Cavalry killed over one hundred people, mostly women and children.

This did not make the Indians want to surrender.

Why did the Lakota decide they needed a new kind of super-chief?

Four Horns, Sitting Bull's uncle, was worried. Too many Lakota had given up their freedom. The ones who were left had to stick together—more than they had before. They needed one chief who would advise them all. So Sitting Bull was made war chief of all the Lakota. There had never been a chief like this before. Four Horns, speaking for all the Lakota not on reservations, said, "When you tell us to fight, we shall fight. When you tell us to make peace, we shall make peace."

What did the whites think of the Lakota's new chief?

They still didn't understand about chiefs, but the newspapers wrote about Sitting Bull and his band of "hostiles." They thought he was dangerous. Even as super-chief, Sitting Bull still couldn't boss anyone around. But people listened to him. He and Crazy Horse agreed to follow Four Horns's advice: "Be a little against fighting, but when anyone shoots be ready to fight."

CHAPTER 7

How the West Was Lost

Sitting Bull and his family pose with visitors in 1882.

What was Sitting Bull's family like at this time?

Some time after his first wife died, Sitting Bull
married two women, Snow-on-Her and Red Woman.
Unfortunately, just like anywhere, some marriages
don't work out. In the late 1860s Sitting Bull divorced
Snow-on-Her. In 1871 Red Woman became sick and
died. So Sitting Bull lived with his son and two
daughters, his adopted son (One Bull), his mother,

> The Lakota didn't need a lawyer to get divorced. A woman could divorce her husband by putting his clothes and weapons outside the tipi. A man could divorce his wife by beating a drum during a meeting of his warrior society and announcing the separation.

and his sister. In 1872 he married a woman named Four Robes and her sister, a widow named Seen-by-the-Nation, who had two sons. So he then lived with ten other people.

Why did the Plains Indians hate the railroad?

The railroad scared the buffalo—and the railroad company hired people to shoot buffalo to feed their workers. Even worse, people shot the buffalo from the train windows for fun. Usually the trains wouldn't even stop. The sides of the tracks were littered with rotting, stinking buffalo and bones.

The transcontinental railroad had been finished in 1869. In 1871 the railroad company wanted to put in a new branch, right through the lands protected by the 1868 treaty. These lands included a valley where buffalo and other animals liked to graze.

What happened when Lakota fought the railroad?

On August 13, 1872, Sitting Bull, Crazy Horse, and several bands of Lakota were camping together near the Powder River. They were planning a battle against the Crow, but scouts reported U.S. soldiers nearby, protecting railroad surveyors. That night while the chiefs were deciding who to fight—Crows or soldiers—war parties of young Lakota stole horses from the soldiers and began fighting them.

The Lakota and white soldiers fought all the next morning. A holy man had told some young men that if they sang the song he had dreamed, then they would be bulletproof. When the men tried it, they were wounded but not killed. Sitting Bull shouted, "Too many men are being wounded! That's enough!" The holy man suggested that anyone who stopped fighting was a quitter and a coward.

AMERICAN VOICES

66 We kill buffaloes for food and clothing, and to make our lodges warm. . . . See the thousands of carcasses rotting on the Plains. Your young men shoot them for pleasure. All they take from [the] dead buffalo is his tail, or his head, or his horns, perhaps, to show that they have killed a buffalo. . . . You call us savages. What are they? **99**

—**Sitting Bull,** to a newspaper reporter

How did Sitting Bull prove his bravery?

Sitting Bull walked toward the soldiers. He sat on the grass one hundred yards away from them and smoked his pipe. "Any Indians who wish to smoke

with me, come on!"
he called. They didn't
really want to at all,
but four warriors
joined him. They
smoked fast and ran to
safety. Sitting Bull
strolled back to the
other warriors. He called
out, "That's enough! We
must stop!"

And they did—except Crazy Horse, who rode right in
front of all the soldiers. The soldiers shot Crazy
Horse's horse, but he himself wasn't hurt. And that
was the end of the battle.

Did the battle stop the railroad?

No. Fighting stopped for the winter, but the next
summer, in 1873, Custer's Seventh Cavalry arrived.
More Lakota and Cheyenne arrived, too. No one was
winning or losing. One historian says that the
Lakota fired the last shots of the summer. They shot
into the river, scaring a bunch of naked soldiers who
were taking a bath.

How did the battle over the railroad end?

The white soldiers went away. The railroad surveyors
disappeared. The Indians had won—or so they
thought. Really what had happened was that the
U.S. economy was in trouble. Hundreds of banks and
businesses shut down. The economic disaster was
called the "Panic of 1873." No one had any money,
not even the railroad company.

U.S. economic problems and people's anger at the Indians led to the final battles between the Plains Indians and the whites—the war for the Black Hills.

What were the Black Hills?

In the western part of the Great Sioux Reservation were the *Paha Sapa*, the Black Hills. Dark evergreen trees made them look black from far away. The beautiful hills were a place where people could always find food. And the hills were sacred, *wakan*. People went there for visions. But they were also *wakan* because there was always food. They were a place where Wakantanka was especially generous.

The Black Hills were also full of gold.

What did the Lakota think of gold?

The Lakota had showed chunks of gold to a priest many years earlier. He said to bury them and not tell anyone. The Oglala holy man Black Elk said gold wasn't good for anything. It was "the yellow metal that makes white people crazy." Unfortunately the Lakota's protection of the Black Hills made the whites curious. Miners who went there sometimes didn't come back. The 1868 Fort Laramie Treaty said that the hills belonged to the Lakota, but white people wondered what the Lakota were hiding.

When the economic troubles of 1873 put everyone into a panic, the government wanted to find out if the rumors of gold were true. Gold would sure solve some money problems. President Grant put George Armstrong Custer in charge of the exploration team that would see what was really in the Black Hills.

Who was Lieutenant Colonel George Armstrong Custer?

Custer (left) and Russian Grand Duke Alexis at the duke's buffalo hunt

One of the most controversial soldiers in American history, Custer had been a hero for the Union in the Civil War. Although last in his class at West Point, the U.S. Military Academy, he became the youngest general in the Union army, famous for his daring actions in battle. He also liked to be noticed and wore fancy uniforms. In a big parade after the Civil War, he got a lot of attention when his horse got loose and people wondered how such a good horseman could lose control of his animal. After the war Custer was assigned to the Seventh Cavalry to fight Indians. But in 1867 he was suspended for a year for absence from duty.

Like the other soldiers Fetterman and Grattan, Custer did not like to take orders, but the headstrong

Custer was more successful. He won battles and never got hurt. Everyone talked about "Custer's luck." Many Americans called him the "Boy General" because he was made a general when he was just twenty-three. The Indians had another name for Custer. They called him "Long Hair." His long reddish blond curls were hard to miss, especially for Plains Indians.

What was Custer like?

People disagree about that now, and they disagreed while he was alive. The soldiers who served under him called him "Iron Butt" because he could ride horseback all day without getting a sore rear end. (They got sore rear ends.) Older generals thought he was  brave but not very smart. General Sheridan liked him, but many officers didn't. Custer was like those kids who can't stay still for a minute and are always getting into trouble for doing things without thinking about them first. He once put his fist through a glass window trying to punch someone in the nose. Attack first and think about it later: That's how he fought in the Civil War. And that's how he fought the Indians.

He adored fighting. He also loved his wife, Libby, and animals. He had dogs who came to battle with him, a pet porcupine, prairie dogs, a snake, and even a mouse who lived in his inkwell. But he also killed and stuffed so many animals that Libby said their living room was full of glittering glass eyes.

By the time he was fighting Indians, Custer was only a lieutenant colonel. Many soldiers had their ranks lowered after the Civil War because the army was smaller. But to a lot of people he was still the Boy General. He was the charming, beloved hero who would save everyone from those horrible Indians.

What was Custer's job in the Black Hills?

He was supposed to find a place to put a fort and look for gold. He commanded the Seventh Cavalry, foot soldiers, Indian scouts, mapmakers, scientists, and newspaper reporters. He also took along a sixteen-piece brass band riding white horses. (This is not a normal part of a survey team, but it was normal when Custer was around. He liked having a band.)

Custer's team needed 2,400 horses and mules to carry its members and all their supplies. Extra men were required to take care of the animals. The Indians called their path "Thieves' Road."

Why did the Crow and other Indian scouts help the whites?

Because the enemy tribes were still angrier at each other than at the whites.

A Crow chief said, "These are our lands by inheritance. The Great Spirit gave them to our fathers, but the Sioux stole them from us. . . . They have murdered our wives, our children. . . . The great white chief will lead us against no other tribe of red men. Our war is with the Sioux and only them. . . . The Sioux have trampled upon our hearts. We shall spit on their scalps."

Did Custer ever find gold?

He found land so rich and beautiful that the guys in charge of the packing supplies on the mules carried bouquets of flowers.

"I can whip the Indians if I can find them."

Custer said that in 1868. Finding Indians to fight had often been a problem for the army. In 1865 troops were so lost for so long that the soldiers ate their horses. That's why Indian scouts were so important to the army, even for a trip to the Black Hills.

And he found gold. "Gold from the grass roots down," said a newspaper. The news set off a gold rush. Thousands of people—greedy or dead broke—went to the Black Hills to look for gold. Noisy, smelly mining towns grew up in the sacred Black Hills.

AMERICAN VOICES

66 The American people need the country the Indians now occupy; many of our people are out of employment; the masses need some new excitement. . . . An Indian war would do no harm, for it must come sooner or later. 99

—Bismarck (North Dakota) *Tribune*, June 17, 1875

What did the government do about the miners?

President Grant sent in the army and ordered General Sheridan to enforce the 1868 treaty, but it was impossible. U.S. soldiers weren't going to shoot a white man for trespassing on Indian land, and if the soldiers threw the miners out, they just came back. The Lakota killed some miners—though probably not as many as the newspapers said—but that just made whites even angrier at the Indians.

President Grant wanted to solve the problem peacefully if possible, so he offered to buy the Black Hills from the Lakota.

What did the Indians think of this?

By now Red Cloud understood that the government would take what it wanted. He tried at least to get a good price for the land. When the government offered six million dollars for the Black Hills, Red Cloud said the Indians wanted six hundred million. Sitting Bull said, "The Black Hills belong to me. If the whites try to take them, I will fight." The day everyone was supposed to meet, hundreds of Lakota rode in, waving rifles and shouting. A warrior from Crazy Horse's camp rode up chanting:

"Black Hills is my land and I love it
And anyone who interferes
Will hear this gun."

And that was the end of the discussion of buying—
or selling—the Black Hills.

Why did the United States invent a war against the Lakota?

The Lakota wouldn't sell the land, and General
Grant couldn't just ignore a famous treaty. A treaty
was a promise—although in the history of U.S. and
Indian treaties, it was a promise that was always
broken sooner or later.

So President Grant and General Sheridan had a
meeting with the White House cabinet. They didn't
say they wanted to steal the Black Hills. They said
they had to keep the Lakota from fighting against
the whites and friendly Indians like the Crow. They
ordered all the Lakota to report to the Great Sioux
Reservation by January 31, 1876. Any Indian who
didn't go to the reservation would be treated as
"hostile." So the Lakota could either surrender or be
hunted by the army.

Did Sitting Bull and the Lakota go to the Great Sioux Reservation?

When the army messengers told Sitting Bull and the
other chiefs to come to the Sioux reservation on
January 31, the Lakota leaders had no idea what
these white men were talking about.

In the winter each Lakota band stayed mostly in one
camp and tried to stay warm. When messengers
appeared during December blizzards, the hunting
bands must have been confused. They didn't have
the same calendar as the whites. And they couldn't

have kept the appointment even if they'd wanted to. Their horses didn't have enough to eat in winter and weren't strong enough to pull the old people through the snow. Many years later White Bull said, "Maybe, if we had had automobiles, we could have made it."

So, on February 1, 1876, the United States declared war on the "hostiles"—the hunting bands. The Lakota didn't even know there was a war on.

What happened when the United States declared war on the Lakota and Cheyenne?

General Sheridan planned another campaign like his last one: The army would attack the Indians in winter and burn their villages. But this was going to be a bigger campaign. Three groups of soldiers would come from three directions, all moving toward the region where Sitting Bull and the "hostiles" hunted and camped. Custer and General Alfred Terry would march west from Fort Abraham Lincoln. Colonel John Gibbon would march east from Fort Ellis, Montana. General Crook would march north from Fort Fetterman.

What happened to the winter campaign?

It got delayed until summer. Only General Crook was able to even begin on time.

General George Crook was another Civil War general who was now fighting the Indians. Often he won his battles. He had great respect for Indian warriors.

But that didn't help him in March 1876. It was so cold that the soldiers had icicles growing from their beards. After marching for two weeks, Crook sent Colonel James Reynolds and three hundred soldiers into a Cheyenne village at dawn. The warriors struggled out of their tipis and moved almost everyone to safety. Reynolds and his soldiers killed only a few Cheyenne, but they burned the village

and captured the Indians' horses. Then they were driven back by the warriors. That night the Cheyenne recaptured their horses. Crook blamed Reynolds, but General Sheridan realized they couldn't make war in the winter.

Where did the homeless Cheyenne go?

They traveled to the Oglala camp of Crazy Horse. Then they all traveled north to Sitting Bull's camp, the only one big enough to take in that many people in the middle of winter.

What did Sitting Bull do when the army was coming to fight the Indians?

He met with the tribal council. Then he sent out messengers to other winter camps and to reservations. The messengers relayed Sitting Bull's words: "It is war. Come to my camp at the Big Bend of the Rosebud Creek."

During the spring, thousands of people came from the hunting tribes and some from the reservations. The Cheyenne chose a head chief, and the Lakota again chose Sitting Bull to be their head chief.

Sitting Bull advised the young men to steal horses. "Spare nobody," he told them. "If you meet anyone, kill him, and take his horse. Let no one live." This was not a good time to be a white traveler or settler anywhere near the Black Hills.

Did Sitting Bull really think he could win a war against the U.S. Army?

He probably did. Red Cloud had been to Washington, D.C. He understood how many whites there were. Sitting Bull did not. During a treaty talk in 1864, one Lakota said: "The white men are marching around in a ring so that we may see them and be led to believe that there are a great number of them. They cannot fool us. We recognize the same people, and they are too few; we are not afraid of them—we outnumber them."

For all of Sitting Bull's life, the Lakota had been the best warriors in the northern Plains.

Why did Sitting Bull do the Sun Dance in June 1876?

The Lakota often performed this ceremony when they had something difficult to do.

In May Sitting Bull had prayed to the Great Mysterious. It wasn't a war prayer. He prayed for food. He prayed that all the Sioux nation would get along well. Then he promised to perform the Sun Dance and to offer Wakantanka "a scarlet blanket."

That June Sitting Bull kept his promise. After cleaning his body and spirit in the sweat lodge, he sat by the sacred tree. His brother, Jumping Bull, cut fifty tiny pieces of flesh from each of Sitting Bull's arms. His blood flowed, making the scarlet blanket.

Then Sitting Bull danced around the sacred pole, staring at the sun. He danced all day and all night and through half the next day, not eating or drinking. Then he stopped, still staring at the sun. People laid him on the ground and sprinkled water on him.

What was Sitting Bull's most famous vision?

He had heard a voice saying, "I give you these because they have no ears." He looked up and saw white soldiers and some Indians on horseback falling from the sky like grasshoppers, with their heads down and their hats falling off. They were falling right into the Indians' camp.

All the Indians understood what this meant. The white men, who would not listen to them, would be killed right in their camp. The Indians believed that this meant they couldn't lose.

Did Sitting Bull's vision come true?

Not right away. First "Three Stars" Crook marched toward the Indians' camp with 1200 soldiers and 200 Indian scouts. The chiefs had said, "Young men, leave the soldiers alone unless they attack us." The young men didn't, and on June 17 over 1500 Indians attacked Three Stars and his troops by the Rosebud Creek. Sitting Bull could not fight—he could barely lift his arms—but he urged his warriors to fight bravely. They fought all day. Then the Indians went back to their camp.

General Crook said the battle was a U.S. victory because the Indians had retreated at sunset, but he had to retreat himself for six weeks to wait for more troops and supplies. The Indians moved west to mourn their dead and celebrate their victories. They traveled along the banks of a river they called the Greasy Grass, named for grass that ripples like water. History books call it the Little Bighorn River.

How did people know that the Battle of the Rosebud wasn't the victory of Sitting Bull's vision?

In the vision the soldiers were falling right into their camp. But the Lakota and Cheyenne were happy about who was coming into their camp on the Greasy Grass: The Indians from the reservation were coming. Soon there would be between 15,000 and 19,000 Indians, including many warriors. Some people say there were 2,000 warriors, but others say there were 4,000 warriors. We can't know for certain. There were no reporters or television cameras around at Greasy Grass, but it was the most Plains warriors that had ever gathered for a fight.

Often one twin is stronger than the other and the weaker one dies. Twins that lived were *wakan*—another good sign for Sitting Bull.

And two more people had joined the camp: Sitting Bull's wife Four Robes had given birth to twin boys a few weeks earlier.

Standing Holy, Sitting Bull's daughter

CHAPTER 8

The Battle of the Little Bighorn

George Custer, at left, and soldiers shooting at Indians

What happened at the Battle of the Little Bighorn?

That question has kept everyone arguing since June 25, 1876. No one agrees exactly what happened.

But it was something like this: The generals were still hoping that the three groups of soldiers would find the Indians at about the same time, or at least that they would keep the Indians from escaping. When the Indians separated into their small hunting bands, they could just melt away in all directions and disappear. That's what the generals and Custer were most afraid of.

On June 17 Custer, General Terry, and Colonel Gibbon met to discuss their next move against the Indians. (It was the day General Crook was losing a battle, but none of them knew that.) Custer was leading the Seventh Cavalry, and their horses could move faster than General Terry and his cannons and Gatlings (which were very old-fashioned machine guns). Terry offered Custer a few of the Gatlings, but Custer said no. They would slow him down too much. Custer was supposed find the Indians and attack the southern end of their camp. If the plan worked, the Indians would scatter to the north and run right into the big guns of Terry and Gibbon. The attack was planned for June 26.

What went wrong?

As Custer and his men marched away from the meeting on June 22, Gibbon said, "Now Custer, don't be greedy, but wait for us." "No, I won't," answered Custer.

Custer didn't wait. He wouldn't listen to the Indian scouts. For three days the Seventh marched and the scouts read the trails. They told Custer there were more Indians than he thought there were. They said the Lakota had held a Sun Dance and expected to win. "There are not Indians enough in the country to whip the Seventh Cavalry," Custer said.

Custer marched his men all night, until they were falling asleep on their horses and bumping into trees. The next morning, June 25, Custer sent his scouts ahead. They told him there were more Indians in the village than the Seventh Cavalry had bullets. Custer said he couldn't see them. Then the scouts—and Custer's brother—said the Indians had seen the soldiers. They hadn't, but Custer was afraid the Indians would escape after all. He had to attack right away.

How did Custer plan his attack?

Custer still didn't know how big the Indian village was or exactly where it was. Actually, the village stretched for three miles, hidden by hills and trees and bends in the river. So Custer divided his 600 troops into four groups. One would stay behind with the mules and supplies. Major Marcus J. Reno, Major Frederick Benteen, and Custer would each lead 150–250 cavalrymen. Benteen would go south, into the hills by the river, to see if there were any Indians there. (There weren't.)

Custer and Reno marched farther. Then an officer saw Indians galloping on horses. "Here are your Indians, running like devils!" he shouted. Now Custer was sure the Indians were going to escape. He sent Reno across the Little Bighorn River to attack from the south end of the village. Custer said the rest of the troops would "support" him. A little later it became clear that no one knew what that meant.

How did there wind up being two separate battles going on at the same time?

Custer didn't join Reno. He led his troops farther north and attacked the other end of the village.

What happened when Reno attacked the village at the Little Bighorn?

The Indians knew the soldiers were coming, but they weren't expecting an attack in the middle of the day. Some of the children were swimming. Women were gathering wild turnips. Then the column of soldiers appeared. People shouted, "They are charging, the chargers are coming!" Bullets ripped through the walls of Hunkpapa tipis.

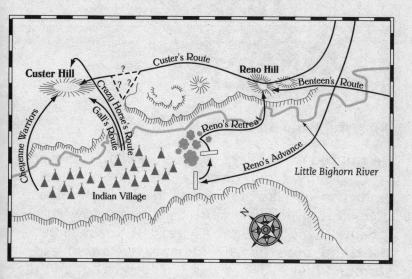

Sitting Bull and One Bull brought their families to safety. Gall was not so lucky. His two wives and three children all were killed. "It made my heart bad," he said later. "After that I killed all my enemies with the hatchet." Sitting Bull gave his own weapons to One Bull. One Bull gave Sitting Bull his guns. Sitting Bull could not fight with a bow and arrow. His arms were still too sore from the Sun Dance, but he could shoot a gun. From horseback he shouted:

"Brave up! We have everything to fight for. If we're defeated, we'll have nothing to live for. It'll be a hard time, but brave up!"

What did Reno do next?

He stopped his soldiers outside the camp. They got off their horses and formed a line, lying on their stomachs to make themselves the smallest targets possible. But "the very earth seemed to grow Indians," Reno said later. Custer was nowhere in sight, and more than 900 Indians were starting to surround them. Also, it was 100 degrees out and the army wore wool uniforms. When the soldiers got off their horses, they shook from tiredness.

Reno later said he "retreated," but it was more of a panicked dash. His men crossed the river again (many getting shot) and got on top of a hill where they could at least see who was shooting at them. And there they stayed. At first hundreds of Indians surrounded them; then most of the Indians went away. Sitting Bull left, too.

Where were the warriors going?

The warriors could see that there was going to be an attack at the north end of the village. They poured across the river and met up with Custer while he was still in the hills above the camp. Sitting Bull went north, too, to protect the women and children who were gathered there. Many of the women and young boys were killing wounded soldiers, but others needed a safe place to wait.

AMERICAN VOICES

66 Indians covered the flat. They began to drive the soldiers all mixed up—Sioux, then soldiers, then more Sioux, and all shooting. The air was full of smoke and dust. I saw the soldiers fall back and drop to the river-bed like buffalo fleeing. **99**

—**Two Moon,** Cheyenne warrior, describing Reno's retreat

What happened to Custer?

When Custer first charged the Indians, he had better guns and more of them. But as his men were killed, the Indians took their guns and ammunition. A Cheyenne woman who was fighting said that bows and arrows were even better than guns in this battle. While a soldier aimed a gun, his enemies could see him. Warriors could stay hidden and fire arrows into the air. Thousands and thousands of arrows rained down on the soldiers.

And, as many people had tried to tell Custer, there were a lot of Indians. They weren't about to run away—which is what Custer had thought he had to worry about—because they were defending their families.

What did Custer do when he realized he was outnumbered?

He sent a message to Benteen to come *fast* and bring ammunition, but Benteen didn't. Custer had to fight with the men he had: 225 of them, including two of his brothers, his sixteen-year-old nephew (who had come "for fun"), and his brother-in-law.

Custer's men never had a chance. They faced probably the two best warriors the Sioux had—Crazy Horse and Gall—and hundreds and hundreds of warriors. Women waved blankets and frightened the soldiers' horses. "The Indians acted just like they were driving buffalo to a good place where they could be easily slaughtered," said an Oglala woman. The battle was over in less than an hour. Every one of Custer's soldiers was dead. By the end of the battle, some witnesses say, soldiers were shooting one another, afraid they would be tortured if the Indians caught them. Only a horse and some young Indian scouts survived. Custer had sent the scouts away before the fighting started. "Custer's luck" had completely failed him.

What was happening to Reno?

He was still stuck on the hill, and it was still hot. Benteen's men showed up at about the time that Custer attacked the other end of the village. So did the supply train. Benteen took over the command of the soldiers on the hill. Reno had lost his hat and, many people thought, maybe his mind. He was a Civil War soldier, but he had never fought Indians before.

Many warriors returned, and for a while Indians and soldiers shot at one another. Some of the soldiers tried to join Custer when they heard the sound of his battle, but the warriors drove them back. The soldiers on the hill used dead horses and piles of saddles to shield themselves from arrows and bullets. They wondered why Custer hadn't come to help them. Then it got too dark to see, and most of the Indians went back to their families. Sitting Bull came to see what was happening and then went to his lodge. The warriors were doing fine.

How did the battle on Reno's Hill end?

The soldiers were rescued just in time. By the morning of June 26, the soldiers on Reno's Hill were in as much danger from thirst as they were from bullets and arrows. Some were killed trying to get water from the river. Then, around noon, the shooting stopped. Sitting Bull could see General Terry and Colonel Gibbon coming with columns of soldiers and big guns. The warriors could have killed off the soldiers, but Sitting Bull said, "Let them go now so some can go home and spread the news." He still believed that if they won, the United States would leave them free to hunt the buffalo.

What happened when Terry and Gibbon came?

Reno, Benteen, and their surviving troops knew they were safe. But none of them knew what had happened to Custer and his men. Were they still alive? A patrol soon came with the answer to that question. They had found Custer's dead troops and then Custer's body, shot through the head and through the heart. He wasn't scalped. He had cut his hair short and was going bald.

Why is the Battle of the Little Bighorn so famous?

The Indians shocked the nation by killing the beloved Boy General and by overpowering the U.S. Army. In 1876 America celebrated its centennial—or hundredth birthday. The United States was feeling strong. How had those "savage" Indians killed off the great Custer? People said that Custer had fought against 10,000 Indian warriors. People looked for someone to blame.

Generals said Custer should not have split his troops into four parts and attacked early. They said Major Reno and Major Benteen should have come to Custer's rescue. (One of Reno's men said that if Reno hadn't been a coward, they'd all be dead.)

The battle is famous because people painted pictures of it that hung in public places across America, showing the heroic white people battling the terrible Indians.

And it is famous because it was the last big fight between Plains warriors and the U.S. Army. It was the Indians' biggest victory, but it turned out to be their biggest loss.

Why did so many whites say Sitting Bull killed Custer?

People blamed him because they wanted to believe that only someone powerful and famous could have killed the great Custer. Newspapers even said Sitting Bull was a white man who had graduated from West Point. In fact, no one knows for sure who killed Custer. Most of the Indians didn't even recognize him.

Whites also thought Sitting Bull was the general in charge of the battle. He wasn't. The Indians don't have generals, and Gall and Crazy Horse were the battle leaders. But pictures of the battle drawn by warriors show Sitting Bull at the center of the battle, with Crazy Horse. He wasn't actually at the center of the fighting, but he was the center for his people. He had had the Sun Dance vision of victory to give them courage, and he could feed them. Sitting Bull had brought the different tribes and bands together.

What did the U.S. Congress do after the Battle of the Little Bighorn?

Congress said that the Indians had to give up the Black Hills and the lands they'd been hunting on. If the Indians didn't sign a new treaty, Congress would not send food to the reservations. This was so unfair that even some of the commissioners at the reservations said they were ashamed. Red Cloud tried to argue, but he and the other Lakota on the reservation had to sign. It was that or starve. The United States had finally managed to steal the Black Hills.

AMERICAN VOICES

66 They made us many promises, more than I can remember, but they never kept but one; they promised to take our land and they took it. 99
—An old man at the Pine Ridge Reservation

66 The government made treaties, gave presents, made promises, none of which were honestly fulfilled. We took away their country and their means of support, broke up their mode of living, their habits of life, introduced disease and decay among them, and it was for this and against this they made war. 99
—General Sheridan, 1878

What happened to the Indians who weren't on the reservations?

The army hunted them down. All through the winter, the army attacked Lakota and Cheyenne wherever they could find them. General Sheridan had more than 9000 soldiers to fight with—about half the U.S. Army. He had all the famous Indian-fighting generals to help him. General Sheridan wanted the Indians on the reservations—or dead. He once said, "The only good Indians I ever saw were dead."

In the months that followed the Little Bighorn, there were many dead Indians. The soldiers killed some. Others starved or froze to death. By the spring of 1877, even Crazy Horse surrendered, bringing his Oglala to Fort Robinson. Sitting Bull and about 300 Hunkpapa crossed the border to Canada to join Sitting Bull's old uncle, Four Horns. The Indians knew Canada as "Grandmother's land," named for Queen Victoria of England.

CHAPTER 9

The Last Indian

The great warrior Sitting Bull

Was life any better when the Lakota got to Canada?

Soon after Sitting Bull arrived, a white man rode right into his camp. He was from the Royal Northwest Mounted Police, which was the police force Canada had created to keep the peace among the Indians. His name was James Walsh, and he was probably the best white friend Sitting Bull ever made.

Walsh told Sitting Bull the laws the Hunkpapa would have to follow—the same rules for people of all races. No shooting people, not even enemy tribes. No horse stealing. They couldn't go back to the United States. But they could keep their guns and horses and hunt the buffalo.

Was the United States glad to have Sitting Bull in Canada?

You might think they'd be glad to have Sitting Bull out of their hair, but they weren't. They were afraid Sitting Bull would gather his warriors and then come back to fight. And they wanted "Custer's killers" to be punished. They told Canada to send Sitting Bull back to the United States and sent General Terry to invite him back, but Sitting Bull wanted to stay in Canada.

What was happening in the United States?

Bad things. Soon after Sitting Bull arrived in Canada, Crazy Horse was bayoneted to death. The army said Crazy Horse was trying to escape, but the Lakota have never believed it. Then a band of old enemies, the Nez Percé (Pierced Noses), came limping into the Hunkpapa camp in Canada. They were the survivors of an attack by the U.S. Army. "We want to be friends," they said. With tears in his eyes, Sitting Bull said they were no longer enemies. They all had red skin, he said, and they all had had their country stolen. But he could not go back to the United States to fight for their leader, Chief Joseph. So the Nez Percé went back and lost their fight against the army. The army put the survivors on a reservation far from their homes. Many died, including Chief Joseph and his family.

AMERICAN VOICES

66 I will remain what I am until I die, a hunter, and when there are no buffalo or other game I will send my children to hunt and live on prairie mice. 99

—Sitting Bull

What happened to the Hunkpapa living in Canada?

The Canadians kept their promise to protect them. Sitting Bull had time to play with his children. A trader taught him to write his name in English. But it was also a hard time for him. He had failed to protect his people from the U.S. soldiers. Many Indians had died or gone to the reservation.

And there were fewer buffalo all the time. In Canada the Hunkpapa couldn't fight other tribes for better hunting grounds. By 1880 they were running out of food. More and more starving Hunkpapa went to reservations in the United States.

Why did Sitting Bull return to the United States?

After almost all his people had left, Sitting Bull, who had "fed a nation," who had fed all those hungry Cheyenne in the middle of winter, begged Walsh for food. Walsh told him he was a "[rude word] nuisance," and Sitting Bull pulled his gun. Walsh kicked him in the rear end. Both Walsh and Sitting Bull were sorry afterward. They really did like each other, but for Sitting Bull life in Canada had become impossible.

On July 19, 1881, Sitting Bull and 187 Hunkpapa surrendered at Fort Buford, in Montana. People could hardly believe that these were the fierce Indians who had killed Custer. They were dressed in rags—or in nothing at all.

What did Sitting Bull say when he surrendered his rifle at Fort Buford?

A newspaper said he motioned to his son, Crow Foot, to pick up the rifle, and said: "I wish it to be remembered that I was the last man of my tribe to surrender my rifle. This boy has given it to you, and now he wants to know how he is going to make a living."

Other people remember that Sitting Bull said to Crow Foot, "My boy, if you live, you will never be a man in this world, because you can never have a gun or a pony."

The worry about how his son would "make a living" was a serious one. The Hunkpapa were starving. But Sitting Bull was wondering about something else, too. How would his son and the other Indians live without the buffalo, without their horses, without their guns? It is the same question that farmers ask now when their family farms have to be sold. If people give up everything they have known, what will they be? What will their children do?

What did the government do with them?

Sitting Bull was taken by steamboat to Standing Rock Reservation. On the way they stopped in

Bismarck, North Dakota, the first white man's town Sitting Bull had seen. They ate in a fancy hotel. Sitting Bull was impressed by ice cream. How did they get the stuff to freeze when it was so hot out? He saw a train and a pocket watch and learned that the whites divided their days into hours, minutes, and seconds. And he sold his autograph to people who came to stare at him.

At Standing Rock, Sitting Bull saw his people again. Then the authorities took him two hundred miles away, to Fort Randall, where he and his wives and children were prisoners of war. The authorities had promised him he could stay at the reservation, but it was two years before they let him go back to Standing Rock.

What was life like on the reservation?

Strange and hard. Sitting Bull had to live in a log house that shut out the light and sun. He had to farm the land. It wasn't even good farmland. Instead of his beautiful warhorses, he owned boring horses that pulled his plow. Instead of the sacred buffalo, he ate beef, which was tasteless and smelled bad. The men had to wear pants and boots, which hurt.

Twice a month the women went to the agency for sugar, coffee, and salt. The agencies treated the Indians like people being given handouts they didn't deserve. The whites seemed (as usual) to have forgotten the treaties. The government *owed* the Indians money and supplies as payment for the land it had taken. Missionaries wanted the Indians to become Christian and for Sitting Bull to divorce one of his wives. (He said he liked them both.) They said the Lakota couldn't perform the Sun Dance.

There was no way for the people to be Lakota. The Indians were supposed to live like whites—the sooner the better.

What happened to children on the reservation?

Lakota boys who have just arrived at Carlisle Indian School in Pennsylvania (left) and, later, as students (right)

Some of them were sent away to Carlisle and other Indian boarding schools. Children at these schools had to dress like white children. When the teachers cut off the boys' braids, the boys thought their parents had died. Only if a parent died would an Indian male cut off his braids. The children were given new "white" names and made to play white children's games. They hated their itchy woolen underwear.

They learned math, geography, and the history of the whites. (Like how the Pilgrims came to the New World to find religious freedom. But Indians couldn't follow their religion.) They were taught that *they* had no history. If they spoke their own language, the teachers hit them with sticks.

Where did Sitting Bull's children go to school?

On the reservation. He wouldn't let them go away from him into the white man's world. Yet he knew that times were changing. He spoke at the school and told the children to learn everything they were being taught. "You are living in a new path," he said. "We older people need you."

Who was in charge of the reservation?

James McLaughlin was the agent in charge of Standing Rock Reservation. He and Sitting Bull began their argument exactly one day after Sitting Bull arrived there. Sitting Bull wanted to collect the government supplies for his people and give them out. That way he would still be feeding his people, like a chief. McLaughlin told Sitting Bull that he was no longer a chief. McLaughlin had been able to find Lakota chiefs who would do what he wanted them to. With Sitting Bull around, MacLaughlin couldn't be sure who people would listen to.

In his book, *My Friend the Indian*, he says Sitting Bull was a coward. For many years people believed McLaughlin. But McLaughlin also let Sitting Bull travel, deciding that if Sitting Bull was away from the reservation he couldn't stir up trouble. McLaughlin himself had taken Sitting Bull to St. Paul and Minneapolis, Minnesota, where Sitting Bull had seen and been amazed by things like telephones and firehouses. McLaughlin arranged for Sitting Bull to go on tour.

Why did Sitting Bull join the Wild West Show?

It is hard to imagine Sitting Bull agreeing to play Cowboys and Indians. Perhaps he was curious to see more of the white world. He hated what the whites had done to his people, but he liked their inventions. He also liked some of the white people.

Sitting Bull and "Buffalo" Bill Cody

Sitting Bull made friends with "Buffalo" Bill Cody. He was famous as a buffalo hunter for the railroad. He had even killed Indians. Cody put on a traveling show, sort of like a circus, that showed audiences around the country the "Wild West" as everyone liked to imagine it. He put on an exciting show of Plains Indians dancing and whooping war cries and chasing a small herd of buffalo.

111

Cody also showed a version of "Custer's Last Stand." In his version, he said the Indians had just been defending themselves. People in the cities loved it. They screamed. They fainted. They booed the Indians, especially Sitting Bull. Then they asked Sitting Bull for his autograph, which he sold for $1.50 each, a lot of money back then.

But Buffalo Bill Cody and Sitting Bull also shared the same problem. The world they loved no longer existed. There were no more buffalo for Cody to kill. White men told Sitting Bull that he wasn't a chief anymore and made him wear pants. In "Buffalo Bill's Wild West," they could show the world who they had been.

Also, he needed money. He couldn't be a chief if he had nothing to give to people. When Sitting Bull used his Wild West earnings to give feasts, McLaughlin was horrified by his lack of respect for money. Sitting Bull was horrified because whites *didn't* give away money and food. He gave money to children he saw begging in the city streets. He couldn't understand why white people would let children go hungry. The Lakota would share their food until it was gone, and then everyone would go hungry together.

But by the end of the summer of 1885, Sitting Bull was ready to go home. Cities were noisy, and he was tired of being asked questions about the Little Bighorn. Cody gave Sitting Bull a white cowboy hat and the horse he had ridden in the show. It was trained to sit and raise one hoof when it heard gunshots.

What was happening on the reservation?

Sitting Bull's mother died in 1884. One of his daughters and his uncle Four Horns died in 1887. He had a new son in 1887 and a daughter in 1888. He also adopted many orphans. But the people in charge of "civilizing" the Indians decided they had found a way to speed up the process: Instead of having shared lands, each Indian family (father, mother, and children) would have its own land to farm—160 acres, just like white people. This would separate people from the big extended families so important to the Lakota. The Great Sioux Reservation would become six small reservations, and the government would sell thousands of acres of land to white settlers.

What did Sitting Bull think of the plan to take away more Lakota lands?

He couldn't fight with guns anymore, but he fought with words. When the government commission came to Standing Rock, they found only twenty-two men who would agree to sell the land. They needed three-fourths of the men to sign the agreement. Back the commissioners went to Washington, disgusted. Some people said they should just take the land, but the government wanted to acquire it legally.

How did General Crook break up the Great Sioux Reservation?

Crook told the chiefs that the best they could do was get a good price for their land. The whites would take what they wanted, one way or another, as they had with the Black Hills. The Oglala and many other Lakota signed the agreement. But Crook couldn't get enough signatures without the Hunkpapa.

Crook told McLaughlin to *get those signatures*. Even though McLaughlin believed this new treaty was unfair to the Indians, he talked to Hunkpapa leaders when Sitting Bull wasn't around. He told them that if they didn't sign the agreement, he would cut off their food supplies. Then McLaughlin set up a meeting and didn't let Sitting Bull and his followers know about it. When Sitting Bull showed up at the last minute, he was too late to stop the sale of the Great Sioux Reservation.

What did Sitting Bull think of the sale of the reservation?

As Sitting Bull left the meeting, a newspaper reporter asked him what the Indians thought about the loss of their lands. "Indians!" Sitting Bull answered. "There are no Indians left but me!"

What happened after the Great Sioux Reservation was broken up?

Sitting Bull stayed away from the agency and from the whites. General Crook tried to keep his promise that the Indians would have enough land and enough rations, but Congress cut the Lakota's beef ration by almost half. There was no rain from August 1889 to June 1890. The Lakota died of starvation, cold, measles, whooping cough, and flu. They had been on the reservation for ten years. They had nothing to live for. Their old ways were gone. When Sitting Bull handed over his rifle, he had asked the right question: How could his people live?

What was the Ghost Dance?

On January 1, 1889, a Paiute holy man named Wovoka had a vision. He saw the Christian messiah come back to earth as an Indian. The Great Plains would be full of buffalo again. All the Indians who had died would live again, riding horses and hunting buffalo. The Great Mysterious told Wovoka how to get ready for this time: The Indians must not fight anyone and they must do a new dance, the dance of the returning spirits. Many people called it the Ghost Dance.

Wovoka's vision spread among the tribes of the Great Plains. It's not clear if Sitting Bull believed in it. But he was interested in any vision that gave the Lakota hope and reminded them of who they were.

Why did the Ghost Dance frighten the whites?

They didn't understand it. All they knew is that the Indians, who were supposed to be acting like white farmers, were dancing in circles until they fell over and had visions. Also, some of the Lakota dancers wore white shirts painted with special designs. They said these shirts were bulletproof. So the whites decided that the Indians were doing a war dance. The newspapers and McLaughlin blamed Sitting

Bull. McLaughlin wanted Sitting Bull arrested, and he got Congress to agree.

66 These hostile Indians have been starved into fighting, and they will prefer to die fighting than starve peacefully. 99

—**General Miles,** one of the most successful Indian fighters

A meadowlark told Sitting Bull, "Lakota will kill you." Was it right?

Yes. McLaughlin sent Lieutenant Bull Head and his Indian police to arrest Sitting Bull. Although McLaughlin said he didn't want Sitting Bull to be hurt, his orders to the police were, "You must not let him escape under any circumstances." One hundred white cavalry soldiers were waiting to help.

How did Sitting Bull die?

On December 15, 1890, just before dawn, forty-three Indian policemen surrounded Sitting Bull's cabin. Lieutenant Bull Head banged on the door. He and two sergeants went in. "You're under arrest," said Bull Head. Sitting Bull began to get dressed, but the police tried to rush him, grabbing him. They were nervous. Little Soldier, who was one of the police, said afterward, "Sitting Bull was not afraid; *we* were afraid." The police were just young reservation men. Sitting Bull's supporters were old warriors. Sitting Bull said, "This is a great way to do things, not to give me a chance to put on my clothes in winter time."

People were gathering from all directions, shouting insults at the police. Many of them had guns. The police kept pushing Sitting Bull. His adopted brother, Jumping Bull, said, "Let us break camp and move to the agency. . . . If you are going to die there, I will die with you." People were yelling, "You shall not take our chief!" Then Sitting Bull shouted, "I am not going. Do with me as you like! I am not going! Come on! Come on! Take action! Let's go!"

People took action. A man named Catch-the-Bear shot Bull Head. As he fell, Bull Head shot Sitting Bull in the chest. At almost the same moment, Red Tomahawk shot Sitting Bull in the head. Either shot would have killed him instantly.

What happened after the police killed Sitting Bull?

Sitting Bull's men attacked the police. In the middle of the fight, Sitting Bull's gray horse thought he was back in the Wild West Show. When he heard gunfire, the horse sat down and raised one hoof as if to shake hands. People panicked. Had Sitting Bull's spirit entered the horse? In the confusion the police hid in the cabin. There they found the chief's young son, Crow Foot, and shot him.

The cavalry arrived then, and the fighting stopped. Some historians believe the Hunkpapa would not have fought the white soldiers. It was Sitting Bull's arrest by his own people they couldn't stand. Twelve Hunkpapa died, including Jumping Bull, and four policemen. Bull Head died the next day.

Relatives of the dead police mutilated Sitting Bull's body before it was buried in an unmarked grave. The meadowlark had told Sitting Bull the truth.

How did people react to Sitting Bull's death?

Sitting Bull's family, 1891

President Benjamin Harrison was relieved. A newspaper said the president hoped now that Sitting Bull was "out of the way" the problems with the Indians could be solved without more bloodshed. (They weren't.) Sitting Bull's friend James Walsh, no longer a Canadian Mountie, said, "He loved his people and was glad to give his hand in friendship to any man who believed he was not an enemy and was honest with him. . . . [He] was murdered by the nation to destroy the principle he advocated—that no man against his will should be forced to be a beggar."

Sitting Bull may or may not have been murdered, as Walsh said, but he did spend the second half of his life defending a "principle," a deep belief about who his people were and how they should be allowed to live.

What happened to the Lakota after Sitting Bull's death?

Two weeks after Sitting Bull was killed, the Seventh Cavalry caught up with some of his supporters. They had joined with a band of Miniconjou Lakota. The soldiers were supposed to bring the Lakota to the reservation, and the Lakota agreed to go. The soldiers and Lakota were at a place called Wounded Knee. When the soldiers were taking the Lakota's weapons, a gun went off—it might have been by accident—and the Seventh Cavalry started shooting. Three hundred Lakota died that day and in the snowstorm that followed.

The Oglala holy man Black Elk was a boy then. He said later that the killings at Wounded Knee were the end of a dream. And it's true that they were the end of a dream of a free Lakota people. Sitting Bull and the other leaders lost their fight to defend their land against invasion.

But it wasn't the end of the Lakota people. The Lakota are still alive and they are still fighting to be Lakota. After a fifty-year fight, the U.S. Supreme Court said that the government had to pay the Lakota for the theft of the Black Hills. The Lakota won't take the money. They want the land. But some Lakota are buying parts of the Black Hills so there will be places to hold ceremonies.

In 2001 there were more Indians and buffalo on the Great Plains than there had been since the late 1870s. The land really wasn't very good for farms and cattle, so people are allowing millions of acres to turn back into prairie. Three hundred thousand buffalo are munching the prairie, and Indian colleges now teach bison (buffalo) management.

The Lakota have worked to keep their traditions alive. Like many native peoples they have learned to live in two worlds and to take what they need from each. They do the Sun Dance and other dances and speak Lakota (and English). People earn their eagle feathers for new kinds of coups, new victories, like graduating from college. They get "war shirts" for excellence in sports and in schoolwork.

Sitting Bull fought for a way of life that he loved. Now his family and the rest of the Lakota say, "We are still here."

Three Sioux photographed by Edward S. Curtis

Note to reader: A question mark means that the date is what we think is true, but we can't be sure.

1803–1806 Lewis and Clark explore the Louisiana Territory.

1820s The train is invented.

1830 The Indian Removal Act legalizes the forced removal of tribes from lands.

1831? Sitting Bull is born.

1837 Smallpox kills most of the Mandan nation (smallpox epidemics in 1818, 1845, and 1850, too).

1841? Sitting Bull kills his first buffalo.

1842 The first covered wagons travel the Oregon Trail to the West.

1845? Sitting Bull scores his "first coup."

1848 Gold is discovered in California, leading to the Gold Rush.

1850 California becomes a state.

1851 The first Fort Laramie Treaty is signed by the Santee (eastern) Sioux.

1852? The Strong Hearts Society makes Sitting Bull a war chief.

1854 Lieutenant John Grattan and his soldiers are killed.

1855 Colonel William S. Harney and his troops destroy the Brulé Lakota camp.

1861   The U.S. Civil War begins.

1862   The Homestead Act promises 160 acres
       of land in the Great Plains to white
       settlers.

1862   President Abraham Lincoln signs the
       law that will create a railroad all the
       way across the country.

1862   The Minnesota uprising by the Santee

1863   The Bozeman Trail opens as a shortcut
       to the Montana goldfields; Red Cloud
       and the Oglala Lakota begin the fight
       against the trail.

1864   Massacre at Sand Creek

1864   Sitting Bull's first battle against the U.S.
       Army

1865   The U.S. Civil War ends. The Thirteenth
       Amendment to the U.S. Constitution
       frees the slaves.

1866   Eighty-one soldiers die in the
       Fetterman Battle.

1868   The Second Fort Laramie Treaty creates
       the "Great Sioux Reservation."

1869? Sitting Bull becomes the chief of the
       Teton Lakota.

1874   Gold is discovered in the Black Hills.

1876   The Battle of the Little Bighorn (also
       known as the Battle of Greasy Grass or
       Custer's Last Stand)

1877 Sitting Bull flees to Canada.

1881 Sitting Bull returns to the United States.

1885 Sitting Bull travels with Bill Cody's Wild West Show.

1889 The Great Sioux Reservation is broken into six smaller reservations.

1890 Sitting Bull is killed.

1890 Massacre at Wounded Knee

1890–1910 The Indian population reaches its low point of fewer than 250,000.

1914–1918 World War I. Many American Indians enlist, fight, and die.

1924 Native people in the United States are given the right to vote, and Congress passes the Indian Citizenship Act, giving American citizenship to all native-born American Indians who have not yet obtained it.

SELECTED BIBLIOGRAPHY

Brown, Dee. *Bury My Heart at Wounded Knee: An Indian History of the American West.* New York: Holt, Rinehart & Winston, 1970.

Connell, Evan S. *Son of the Morning Star.* New York: Promontory Press, 1993.

*Freedman, Russell. *Children of the Wild West.* New York: Clarion, 1983.

Greene, Jerome A., ed. *Lakota and Cheyenne: Indian Views of the Great Sioux War, 1876–1877.* Norman: University of Oklahoma Press, 1993.

*Grutman, Jewel H., and Gay Matthaei. Adam Cvijanovic, illustrator. *The Ledgerbook of Thomas Blue Eagle.* West Palm Beach, Fl.: Lickle Publishing, 1999. (reprint of 1994 ed. published by Thomas Grant.)

Hassrick, Royal B. *The Sioux: Life and Customs of a Warrior Society.* Norman: University of Oklahoma Press, 1964.

Hutton, Paul Andrew, ed. *The Custer Reader.* Lincoln: University of Nebraska Press, 1992.

*Isaacs, Sally Senzell. *America in the Time of Sitting Bull: The Story of Our Nation from Coast to Coast, 1840–1890.* Des Plaines, Il.: Heinemann Library, 2000.

*Marrin, Albert. *Sitting Bull and His World.* New York: Dutton, 2000.

*Sandoz, Mari. *These Were the Sioux.* New York: Hastings House, 1961.

Utley, Robert M. *The Lance and the Shield: The Life and Times of Sitting Bull.* New York: Henry Holt, 1993.

Vestal, Stanley. *Sitting Bull, Champion of the Sioux.* 2d ed. Norman: University of Oklahoma Press, 1957.

Walker, James R. *Lakota Belief and Ritual.* Raymond J. DeMallie and Elaine A. Jahner, eds. Lincoln: University of Nebraska Press, 1980.

* For young readers

Page 7, D. F. Barry, Library of Congress; page 15, Library of Congress; page 18, Frank B. Fiske, National Anthropological Archives, Smithsonian Institution/(3179-B6); page 28, Edward S. Curtis, Library of Congress; page 30, shield, about 1870, unknown Sioux artist, Denver Art Museum Collection: gift of C. W. Douglas, 1932.237, © Denver Art Museum 2003; page 32, courtesy, Colorado Historical Society, CHS-X3076; page 40, Library of Congress; page 43, National Anthropological Archives, Smithsonian Institution/(NAA INV 08590700, Ms 1929-b); page 53, Library of Congress; page 58, Library of Congress; page 65, AV1990.32.34, Carl Ludwig Boeckmann, Minnesota Historical Society; page 67, Library of Congress; page 68, Joseph A. Kern, Library of Congress; page 75, courtesy, Denver Public Library Western History Collection, X-31937; page 80, Library of Congress; page 91, D. F. Barry, Library of Congress; page 92, Frederic Remington, Library of Congress; page 104, courtesy, Denver Public Library Western History Collection, Nate Salsbury, NS-102; page 109 (left), courtesy, Denver Public Library, X-32086; page 109 (right), National Anthropological Archives, Smithsonian Institution/(NAA INV 06819400); page 111, Library of Congress; page 118, D. F. Barry, Library of Congress; page 120, Edward S. Curtis, Library of Congress. Maps on pages 10, 70, and 95 by Patricia Tobin.